Little

Living with Early Infant Loss

Glenda Mathes

LITTLE ONE LOST

Living with Early Infant Loss

Reformed Fellowship, Inc.
3500 Danube Drive SW
Grandville MI 49418

Little One Lost: Living with Early Infant Loss

Send requests for permission to quote from this book to:

Reformed Fellowship, Inc.
3500 Danube Dr. SW
Grandville MI 49418
Phone: (616) 532–8510
Web: www.reformedfellowship.net
Email: office@reformedfellowship.net

Book design by Jeff Steenholdt

Printed in the United States of America

ISBN: 978-1-935369-05-9

This book is dedicated to the brave families who relived their loss and shared their pain in the hope of helping others.

He will tend his flock like a shepherd;

he will gather the lambs in his arms;

he will carry them in his bosom,

and gently lead those that are with young.

—*Isaiah 40:11*

Contents

Preface

This book grew from an article about infant loss that I wrote for the publication *Christian Renewal* (May 12, 2003). The article wasn't my idea, and it wasn't one I wanted to write. As I received suggestions and information regarding infant loss, I resisted the idea. Like Saul, who became Paul, I kicked against the goads (Acts 26:14). I was reluctant to write the article because I didn't want to revisit my own miscarriage experience, but I didn't understand the root of my reluctance or how I used denial to cope with the reality of my guilt and grief until I began writing this book. And I began writing this book because, after the *Christian Renewal* article appeared, several women who had suffered miscarriages contacted me. One related how she, her mother, sisters, and aunts cried together around the kitchen table as they discussed the article and their personal experiences with loss. She wrote, "Thank you for finally giving us permission to grieve."

My own mother asked, "Did you know that I had a miscarriage?" That knowledge had lain dormant, buried under vague childhood memories, but her question made the knowledge quicken. A seed began to germinate. The seedling took root and grew into a strong tree of conviction regarding the need for a book addressing the issue of early infant loss from a biblical perspective.

I am using *early infant loss* as a general and gentle term to refer to miscarriage, stillbirth, and the death of a newborn. In a general sense, *early infant loss* can be used handily as concise and comprehensive shorthand for these various losses. In a gentle sense, *early infant loss* can be used as sensitive and sympathetic language for these painful losses. Many terms associated with infant loss have been hijacked by pro-abortion rhetoric. When words have acquired negative connotations or seem insensitive, this book deliberately uses alternatives. I use the word *miscarriage,* even though it is sometimes considered an outdated layman's term, in preference to the medical term *spontaneous abortion.* It seems heartless to use a phrase that associates the unanticipated loss of miscarriage with the intentional act of abortion. Some parents suffering loss may be unpleasantly surprised and additionally distressed by medical terms used during their experience. For more definitions and the sensitive use of terms, see the appendix in the back.

While much of this book may be applied to the loss of a child through Sudden Infant Death Syndrome (SIDS) or a loss at any stage of life, the focus is on early infant loss. This focus is not due to a difference in significance, but because much has already been written about later loss, and its significance is more commonly acknowledged. Early infant losses, on the other hand, are not always considered significant. Yet they can be no less traumatic for parents, especially mothers. These losses run the gamut of human experience and emotion. They can be a brief incident that barely affects the mother or a harrowing experience that continues to haunt her. The chronic ache of infertility is often an unacknowledged loss. These are all losses of a child the parent never really knew. People often do not know how to respond to such losses.

Many women who experience early infant loss don't talk about it. And many of the people around them prefer it that way. It's difficult to know how to comfort or even *whether* to comfort a parent who has lost an infant at a very early stage of life. In many cases, the earlier the loss, the less significant it seems, and the less it is discussed.

That brings me to the *biblical perspective* I mentioned earlier. I use the term *biblical perspective* to mean a mindset that embraces God's Word, the Bible, as the primary guide for all of life's activity and thought. A *biblical mindset* is planted in God's Word, nurtured by continual prayer, and pruned by God's providence. It also is progressively renewed by God's Word (Rom. 12:2) and re-formed to Christ's image (2 Cor. 3:18). That is why the reader will find many biblical references throughout this book. I believe the most biblical and robust expression of Christianity is the Reformed faith. Its emphasis on God's sovereign providence and His covenantal love marvelously comfort and sustain believers as they are buffeted by life's trials and tempests. It is my prayer that God will use this book to increase awareness of the significance of early infant loss, to grant those who have suppressed their loss the freedom to grieve, to comfort grieving parents and other family members, and to assist many in ministering to those who grieve a "little one lost."

Part One: Acknowledging Our Loss

1: The Hole in My Heart

An elderly woman tirelessly knits another tiny afghan. A middle-aged woman carefully arranges pictures and ribbons in a beautiful scrapbook. A young woman tenderly pats soil around a young tree being planted in her yard. What do these different women and their various activities have in common?

The knitting, pasting, and planting are ways these three women cope with the loss of a pre-term infant who never felt soft yarn, never wore satin ribbons, and never saw green leaves glow translucently in the sun. The unfulfilled anticipation of new life lost before birth—like a tender bud pinched by an early frost—is what makes the loss of a pre-term infant so piercing. Yet society often minimizes such loss. We live in an abortion-accepting society that has hardened its collective heart to the loss of prenatal life. Why mourn the loss of a "fetus"? Medical professionals in the recent past took away the baby without allowing the mother to see it. Even Christians sometimes minimize infant loss. Insensitive comforters say, "At least you can have other children." Mothers are expected to "get over it." Fathers are frequently ignored, hovering on the fringe while friends focus on the grieving mother.

For those who believe that life begins at conception, a loss at any point in the pregnancy is significant. Even the loss of the littlest one is the loss of a real person. Each child is unique, created in God's image. Such a loss rips a hole in the parent's heart and leaves an aching void. No other child can completely fill the jagged hole or smooth its scarred edges. The parent's heart will always ache for the lost child.

There's a hole in my heart.

My husband and I have four wonderful adult children; I am thankful every day that they all love the Lord and walk in His ways.

But we also have a tiny child in heaven. Before our marriage, we discussed having children. At the time, we talked about the possibility of two children by natural birth and—if we wanted more—two by adoption. As we progressed in our marital journey and matured in our spiritual walk, we learned more about submitting our wills to the Lord. We left the number of our children and the method for bringing them into our family more and more in the Lord's hands.

God blessed us with two little boys about two-and-a-half years apart. We thought God's provision was perfect and were content with two sons. But as our sons grew, we found ourselves longing for another child. We longed longer. Eventually, we learned we were expecting our third child. Unanticipated problems arose during that pregnancy. My doctor could no longer hear the baby's heartbeat. He told me to go home and wait. We waited. We became resigned to what we believed was the inevitable loss of our child.

But something unexpected happened. We didn't lose the baby. A visit to the doctor indicated that the baby seemed to be growing, and eventually the doctor once more heard the baby's heartbeat. We were thrilled with the hope of a full term baby, but we also were prepared for the possibility of welcoming into our home a child who was handicapped.

When a healthy daughter was born, we could hardly believe God's goodness! Not only were we blessed with a healthy baby, but also— after two boys—our baby was a little girl! As I dressed her in a tiny pink dress and bonnet before leaving for church on her first Easter Sunday, my heart overflowed with thankfulness.

My full heart made me begin to believe that my quiver was full, too. My husband began to feel the same way. We were surprised to discover a year later that we were expecting another child. I confess that I had difficulty adjusting to the idea. My spirit was far from submissive. With three young children, I felt I was busy enough. I didn't rail or complain to God, but I wasn't rejoicing or thanking Him either. Eventually I came to the point of grudging acceptance. I was able to smile as I told family members about our anticipated child.

Then suddenly I was no longer pregnant. There were no warning signs to prepare me. There was no waiting and coming to terms. Just when I had finally accepted my pregnancy, it disappeared. It was very early in the pregnancy, and I began to question if I had actually been pregnant. Perhaps it was just an extremely late cycle.

It is only now, over twenty years later, that I realize to what extent I used denial to deal with my grief and guilt. Notice how I described my loss? "I was no longer pregnant" and "my pregnancy disappeared." My descriptors are indicators of my perception. I didn't think of it as a baby. I didn't even think of it as a miscarriage. I told myself that I probably hadn't been pregnant. Denying the pregnancy's existence helped me deal with the guilt I felt over my initial reluctance in accepting it. Denial was my crutch.

But my perspective about our family had changed. I no longer felt that our quiver was full; I longed for another child. My husband was also eager for another child.

When we discovered a year later that I was again pregnant, my response was genuinely joyful and thankful. A second healthy daughter was born full term. Whenever the nurses brought her to my husband and me, we took off the hospital's pink stocking cap to marvel at her fuzzy, pale hair. After she came home with us, I loved brushing her hair into its natural waves. Now, in addition to two handsome sons, we had two beautiful daughters: one with brown eyes and dark curls and the other with blue eyes and blonde waves.

People told us we had a "million-dollar" family. We'd never before heard the phrase—used to refer to a family with two boys and two girls—but heard it often when our children were little. We believed it originated in the idea that a pair of sons and a pair of daughters were worth a million dollars. After we began paying tuition for all four of our children to be enrolled in private Christian schools, however, we joked about our new understanding of the phrase! During all those busy years, with their joyful blessings and their heartrending struggles, I suppressed the truth about my loss. I was pregnant. I lost a baby.

There is a hole in my heart.

2: Society's Paradox

The experience that created the hole in my heart can't begin to compare with the wounds many others have endured. Some women have miscarriages similar to mine, but many others experience excessive bleeding and even shock in far more traumatic losses. Some enter the hospital. Some clearly see the still form of their tiny child.

Some moms carry their child full term, feeling kicks and turns, hearing heartbeats at doctor appointments, naming the child and preparing the nursery, only to realize suddenly that the baby is not moving. A doctor confirms the baby's death. These poor mothers must go through the agonizing experience of labor and delivery, knowing that at the end—instead of the joyful bonding anticipated for so many months—their aching arms will cradle a lifeless child.

Other moms go through a normal pregnancy and labor until something abruptly goes wrong during delivery. The baby's heartbeat stops. Frantic action ensues. The festivity of the delivery room transforms into the devastation of a lamentation chamber.

Others, holding their tiny son for the first time, watch him take his last breath. Still others bring a healthy daughter home to bond with the entire family, only to wake one morning and discover her cold body lying motionless on the crisp, new sheet.

The experiences and circumstances may differ, but they share the commonality of loss. The loss of a child through miscarriage, the loss of a child through stillbirth, or the loss of a newborn child is the loss of a real person. Parents faced with such a loss may hardly know what to think, how they should feel, what they should say, or what they ought to do. Caregivers and counselors are generally becoming more sensitive to some forms of infant loss than in the past, but family members or friends may feel just as confused as the parents. Those who don't know what to say may feel that it is better not to say anything. The loss is often ignored; the grief is often suppressed. Few parents feel free to discuss the loss of miscarriage with others. They may feel—and others may believe—that it is better to ignore the loss and simply go back to the business of getting on with life.

When it comes to infant loss, we live in a split-personality society. On the one hand, parents expect the healthy birth of a child as a foregone conclusion. On the other hand, some mothers accept the horrible death of a child through abortion as a legitimate right.

One mother wrote to me about the "shock" of infant loss. It is indeed a shock to lose an infant in our technologically advanced culture, which views a safe delivery and a healthy baby as the norm. Our culture anticipates that children will outlive parents. At the same time, legalized abortion has numbed society's conscience to the point that it accepts murder as a personal prerogative. Abortion rhetoric has so hijacked public discourse that the entire discussion of infant loss has been tainted by its terms. In both ways, our society wears blinders.

A full-term pregnancy and healthy birth aren't as common as many think. Within fairly recent history, infant mortality was astoundingly prevalent. And one might be surprised to learn the high incidence of miscarriage and full-term loss today. We should not automatically expect a problem-free pregnancy and the full-term birth of a healthy baby.

But one also needs to guard against accepting abortion rhetoric and using its terms. The legalization of abortion has created a warped view of prenatal life that denies its personhood. What is called a "product of conception" or "fetal tissue" is really a child with a soul. Covenant Transport has it right with the profound proverb that appears on the back doors of their trucks: "It is not a choice. It is a child." This is the paradox: the expectation of a healthy birth and the acceptance of a horrible death coexist in the same society. With both an idealistic expectation of complication-free birth and a perverse view of prenatal life, is it any wonder that parents are shocked or confused by infant loss?

Although a mother suffering a miscarriage had less time to bond with her child than a mother who lost a baby near its due date, a miscarriage can be extremely shocking and confusing. The shock and confusion are complicated by society's unspoken tradition not to speak about miscarriage. Many older women suffered from that tradition and never felt free to grieve. Even today, women rarely discuss their miscarriages with others. Traditional taboos remain tenaciously ingrained.

Society's paradox and traditional taboos can be overcome only when our society as a whole and its citizens as individuals realize that life is a gift from God. Each child's development in the womb is His marvelous and creative work. He brings each child to life and He takes each person to death at His appointed time. He is the giver of life in the womb, and He alone must be the taker of it.

God doesn't promise that life will be free from struggle. In fact, He promises just the opposite. Christ tells believers, "In this world you will have tribulation." He adds, however, "But take heart; I have overcome the world" (John 16:33). Life isn't always good or always beautiful. Too many parents fail to think beyond the pastel paint of the nursery walls. Life is full of struggle. They and their precious little children will certainly experience some amount of it.

But parents can take heart. They can bring children into the world, knowing that Christ has overcome the world, and God will keep His children safe. No one can snatch believers from Christ's hand (John 10:28). The name of each and every child of God is engraved on the palms of His hands (Isa. 49:16).

The following poem reflects these eternal truths.

Knitting

I view the labor of love's hands
through lenses veiled in teary mists
and think of life as it is now—
uncertain, nebulous—who knows
what ill might lie ahead? Hope fails.
I whisper prayers for your chosen name.

So many casts! I cannot name
the countless things these gnarled, old hands
have knit. My passing memory fails
to find sought objects in the mists
of younger times. God only knows
all the lost and forgotten now.

I've counted knitted stitches, now
I count the purls. I've learned to name
sweet blessings, but who always knows
the bitter ones? The gracious hands
that nourish with life-giving mists
will trim the fruit tree if it fails.

The dropped stitch is the one that fails
to do its useful purpose now.
It disappears in empty mists
where no one can recall its name—
leaving a hole not ripped by hands—
without a soul who cares or knows.

I have a friend who thinks she knows
exactly how to knit. She fails
to see the needles in her hands
as weapons that are useful now
to shape the vague into its name
and save it from the unknown mists.

My needles dance. A brief tear mists
in my reflecting eye. It knows
the scope of pain knit in a name:
hard tests, bare passes, and harsh fails.
I smooth the cheering softness now
of small shawl shape in trembling hands.

In future mists my eyesight fails,
but one who knows you even now
has your name graven on his hands.

—Glenda Mathes

3: Knit Together

The concept for the poem "Knitting" is based on a well-known and dearly loved Scripture text, a text that has become a familiar rallying verse for those who in recent decades have become active in promoting the value of life in the womb. Guided by God's Spirit, David—who knew infant loss—writes, "For you created my inmost being; you knit me together in my mother's womb" (Ps. 139:13, NIV84). This verse and its context in Psalm 139 clearly convey the personhood of a child in the womb. That is why it has become so popular within the pro-life movement. But it is not the only pro-life verse in the Bible. The complete scope of Scripture—from creation to consummation—assumes the personhood of every human, including the unborn child.

God crowned His creative endeavors when He created man in His own image and granted him a soul. God said, "Let us make man in our image, after our likeness" (Gen. 1:26). The Lord formed man from the dust of the earth, breathed into his nostrils the breath of life, and he became a living soul (Gen. 2:7). Being created in God's image is a foundational fact that elevates humankind above all other life on earth.

After God blessed Adam and Eve, He commanded them, "Be fruitful and multiply and fill the earth and subdue it and have dominion over the fish of the sea and over the birds of the heavens and over every living thing that moves on the earth" (Gen. 1:28). Adam and Eve understood their superiority and stewardship over all the other creatures God had made. They also understood their responsibility to have children.

From the very first childbirth, there was an awareness of its astonishing character. When Eve delivered her first son, she said, "With the help of the LORD I have brought forth a man" (Gen. 4:1,

NIV84). Humanity's first mother acknowledged God's role in the mystery of childbirth. Her labeling him as a "man" indicates her acceptance of this helpless newborn as fully human and fully valuable, created—as she and Adam had been—in the image of God. Christ affirms the value of human life over that of other creatures when he assures believers that they are more valuable than the birds of the air (Matt. 6:26; 10:29–31).

Because all people are created in God's image, they all—including children not yet born—have value. Job acknowledges the common status he shares with a child in the womb, since they were both created by the same God: "Did not he who made me in the womb make him? And did not one fashion us in the womb?" (Job 31:15). The unborn child shares in the human characteristic of reflecting God's image.

Each individual becomes a person in the womb. Although we may not understand the complexities of human development or the mystery of how God unites soul and body, we can be certain that life begins at conception when soul and body are united. Consider Ecclesiastes 11:5, "As you do not know the path of the wind, or how the body is formed in a mother's womb, so you cannot understand the work of God, the Maker of all things" (NIV84). The teacher equates the mystery of the wind's way with the mystery of the unborn's development, and compares those mysteries to the Creator God's work. The New King James Version is more specific regarding the formation of a baby in the womb, talking about "how the bones grow." Some other versions merely imply the union of body and soul (although sometimes specified in footnotes), but the English Standard Version clearly portrays that union: "As you do not know the way the spirit comes to the bones in the womb of a woman with child, so you do not know the work of God who makes everything."

How the body and soul unite within the pre-born child is a mystery, but *that* they unite is a biblical given. The Old Testament overflows with additional affirmations of the pre-born child's personhood. Jacob and Esau were viewed as distinct individuals before birth (Gen. 25:22–28). Special directives protected the child in a pregnant mother's womb (Ex. 21:22–25). And Samson was consecrated from his mother's womb (Judg. 13:2–5).

In addition to the Psalm 139 text noted earlier, David often wrote of the unborn as a person. His confession of sin in Psalm 51 implied personhood that existed from the moment of conception: "Behold, I was brought forth in iniquity, and in sin did my mother conceive me" (v. 5). In Psalm 22, David spoke of God's relationship with him from and before birth: "On you was I cast from my birth, and from my mother's womb you have been my God" (v. 10). David did not distinguish between prenatal and natal stages of infancy. He was a person in God's sight before as well as after his birth. This is a reflection of God's own attitude. When He metaphorically speaks of His people as a person in Isaiah 46:3, God does not differentiate between the unborn and the born: ". . . who have been borne by me from before your birth, carried from the womb."

God has plans for persons before their birth. He told Jeremiah, "Before I formed you in the womb I knew you, and before you were born I consecrated you" (Jer. 1:5). Isaiah, another Old Testament prophet, confessed, "Before I was born the LORD called me; from my birth he has made mention of my name" (Isa. 49:1, NIV84). Isaiah quickly reinforced this concept of prenatal calling by God: ". . . he who formed me in the womb to be his servant" (v. 5). These Old Testament passages clearly demonstrate the personhood of the unborn child, which is bestowed by God.

In addition to the many Old Testament references to the humanity of unborn children, New Testament passages also confirm the personhood of the pre-born. The angel telling Zechariah that his prayer had been heard and that his wife, Elizabeth, would bear a son, added, "and he will be filled with the Holy Spirit, even from his mother's womb" (Luke 1:15). Later this pre-born child leaped for joy in the presence of his Savior, then only a tiny embryo in the womb of *His* mother (Luke 1:41, 44).

The fact that God took on human flesh and came to earth as a child in the womb proclaims not only His identity with humanity, but also the personhood of the unborn. Christ was divine, and John was clearly blessed with a special dispensation of the Spirit, but the biblical record concerning these pre-born infants confirms them as living persons. In fact, the Greek word *brephos*, used to describe the baby in the womb in Luke 1, is the same word used to describe the baby in the manger in Luke 2. When writing this record, Luke—who, as a physician, was knowledgeable about medical matters—intentionally equates a pre-born child with an already-born child.

Romans 9:11–12 illustrates the doctrine of election through the example of Jacob and Esau by echoing Genesis 25, which witnesses to the unique existence of each twin before birth. In Paul's letter to the Galatians, he describes his calling by writing that God "set me apart before I was born" (1:15). Just as Samson had been consecrated before birth in Judges 13, Paul was set apart from his mother's womb.

The significance of these passages cannot be missed. Throughout the Old and the New Testaments, life in the womb is considered equivalent to life outside the womb. The Bible makes it clear that a baby is a baby. From conception to birth, every child is being knit together by the Creator. The loss of a child at any stage of pregnancy, during delivery, or after its birth is a genuine loss that has significance. That's why—in spite of our society's schizophrenia and traditional taboos—it is altogether appropriate to grieve the loss of an infant, whether that loss occurs before, during, or after the baby's birth.

4: Common Occurrence

A biblical understanding of life before birth leads to the inevitable conclusion that early infant loss is significant and may appropriately be grieved. Yet many grieving parents feel very alone. They may not know anyone who has experienced a similar loss. Their friends all seem to carry pregnancies full term with no complications; they sling bulging diaper bags over their shoulders and cradle newborn babies in their arms. The grieving parents' arms—and hearts—remain achingly empty.

Modern medical care and technological advances make it seem as if infant loss is a thing of the past. It's true that losing a child was far more common in earlier history, but infant loss today may be a more common occurrence than most people think. The grieving parent is not alone. Throughout history many a parent has wept beside the grave of a child. In fact, humanity's first parents lost a child. Although that child was an adult murdered by his older brother, the fact remains that the very first parents to walk this earth grieved the loss of a son (Gen. 4).

King David, who wrote so eloquently about a child's amazing development in the womb, was a father who lost a newly born child. When his tiny son became sick, David fasted and prostrated himself before the Lord, praying through the night. In spite of his passionate pleas, the child died on the seventh day after birth. Then David stood up, and one of his first actions—even before eating—was worship. David's loss was in judgment for his sin, but it's important to note that David recognized God's sovereignty in both the giving and the taking of his son's life. He responded to his loss with worship (2 Sam. 12).

John Calvin (born in 1509) married a widow with two children, but he lost the only child of their union when that son was born prematurely and lived a brief two weeks. His grief overflowed when he wrote in a letter to a friend, "God have pity on us!" But—like David—he acknowledged God's sovereignty: "God has indeed dealt us a heavy blow by the death of our son, but He is our Father and knows what is good for His children."[1] In spite of the feeling of helplessness and the grief piercing his heart, Calvin was able to remember and cling to the biblical promises of God's love.

Following the loss of a child, James W. Bruce III was moved to write about Calvin's loss as well as the losses of many other figures from church history in his book, *From Grief to Glory.*[2] Martin Luther, John Bunyan, George Whitfield, Charles Wesley, Horatius Bonar, and Charles Haddon Spurgeon all lost dearly loved little ones.

"We who have lost the company of a child do not go alone," Bruce writes. "We may keep company with these men and their wives as we pass through the Valley of Baca—the Valley of Weeping spoken of in Psalm 84:5–7" (p. 16). Parents who walk through the valley of the shadow of death can know that other godly parents have stumbled through that dark terrain and walked on into the light.

Bruce continues, "Follow them into the Valley of Weeping, but do not stay there. Press ahead! The path that leads to glory is the way of peace" (p. 17). Like Calvin, Bruce stresses that, after the loss of a child, peace is found only in the knowledge that all the events of our lives are for God's glory. All the distresses of this life cannot compare with the glories that await believers. The same Shepherd who leads grieving parents through this dark valley will bring them beside still waters and into peaceful pastures.

Anne Bradstreet, a Puritan and the first true published poet in America,[3] lived in a time when childbirth frequently claimed the lives of mother and infant. After several childless years, she eventually was

---

1. The two quotations from John Calvin's letters are recorded on page 114 of *John Calvin: Genius of Geneva* by Lawrence Penning (Neerlandia, Alberta: Inheritance Publications, 2006).

2. *From Grief to Glory: Spiritual Journeys of Mourning Parents* by James W. Bruce III (Wheaton, Illinois: Crossway Books, 2002). Although the Crossway edition is out of print, the book has been republished by Banner of Truth (*www.banneroftruth.org*). Bruce maintains a website with helpful information for grieving parents: *www.grieftoglory.com*.

3. On page 91 of *Beyond Stateliest Marble: The Passionate Femininity of Anne Bradstreet*, Douglas Wilson speaks of the publication of Bradstreet's first book of poems as "a significant milestone" (Nashville: Cumberland House Publishing, 2001).

able to bring eight children into the world. She wrote a moving poem about the possibility of death as she faced one of those births.[4] She not only faced the fear of death in childbirth but she also knew the pain of loss. Four grandchildren died very early in life, one in a premature birth that also claimed the life of the child's mother. In poetry that transcends time and touches hearts, Bradstreet reflected on the brevity of her grandson's life and the short lives of his two sisters:

> No sooner came, but gone, and fall'n asleep,
> Acquaintance short, yet parting caused us weep;
> Three flowers, two scarcely blown, the last i' th' bud,
> Cropt by th' Almighty's hand; yet is He good.[5]

In spite of her grief over these children's brief lives, Anne Bradstreet was able to affirm that God is in control *and* God is good.

Anne Bradstreet was an early colonist, but immigrants settling America over the next two hundred years experienced the same concerns about childbirth and infant loss. A volume of letters between Dutch immigrants in Iowa and their families in the Netherlands depicts the frailty of life and the common loss of children in the Midwest in the mid-nineteenth century. One family's letters record the trials of a couple who lost an unbelievable twelve out of their fourteen children.[6] Losing twelve out of fourteen children would be considered too unrealistic for fiction, but it actually happened to this family. It is almost beyond modern comprehension, yet the mid-nineteenth century is not that far behind us on the time horizon.

Scripture, poetry, and letters all convey the common experience and the pain of infant loss through the ages up to modern times. This common experience happened not only to me but also to my mother.

"Did you know I had a miscarriage?" my mother asked me after she read my article in *Christian Renewal.*

---

4. "Before the Birth of One of Her Children" is found on pages 40–41 in the section on Anne Bradstreet in *Early American Poetry,* edited by Jane Donahue Eberwein (Madison, Wisconsin: University of Wisconsin Press, 1978).

5. The poetry quotation is the first part of "On My Dear Grandchild Simon Bradstreet, Who Died on 16 November, 1669, Being But a Month, and One Day Old" (pp. 55–56) in *Early American Poetry.*

6. The letters, compiled by John Stellingwerff and translated from the Dutch by Walter Lagerwey, appear in *Iowa Letters: Dutch Immigrants on the American Frontier,* edited by Robert P. Swierenga (Grand Rapids, MI: William B. Eerdmans, 2004).

"Yes," I said slowly, realizing that I had never asked her about it. I remembered her telling me many years earlier that her first pregnancy had ended in miscarriage.

"They took the baby away without letting me see it," she told me with tears in her eyes. "'Forget it!' they said. 'Just forget about it. You'll get over it.'"

The miscarriage I heard about was in 1949; the tears I witnessed were in 2003.

More recently an older woman told me that her seventh child miscarried in a hospital in the 1960s. She was told that the baby was deformed and she was never permitted to see it.

"That was a mistake," she said quietly.

In the recent past, miscarried and even stillborn infants were whisked away by hospital personnel before mothers or fathers could see the baby. Parents were encouraged to forget about the child and go on with life. Grief was suppressed.

If you have suffered such a loss, you are far from alone. Miscarriage estimates vary from fifteen to twenty or more percent of pregnancies before twenty weeks. Losses after twenty weeks through stillbirths are variously estimated as one percent or seven out of one thousand. The Wisconsin Stillbirth Service Program website indicates that one stillbirth occurs in about every 115 births.[7]

Although parents who lose these littlest children may feel very alone, the truth is that they are in a great company. Our first parents and parents through the ages have felt the keen edge of grief from losing a child. Many parents today continue to grieve the loss of little ones. And many couples grieve the loss of children they were never able to conceive.

In Paul's first letter to the Corinthians, he assures them that every struggle is "common" to humanity and promises: "God is faithful" (1 Cor. 10:13). God will not try you beyond your ability but will equip you to cope with every trial. He will enable you to endure even the heartrending loss of your little child.

---

7   Grieving parents as well as counselors can find helpful information at the Wisconsin Stillbirth Service Program website (*www2.marshfieldclinic.org/wissp*).

Part Two: Losing a Child

5: Repeated Loss

Although many grieving mothers and fathers feel isolated in their grief, early infant loss has been a frequent occurrence throughout history and continues to be common today. It can help grieving parents to know they are not alone. That is especially true for couples—like Scott and Patsy—who have struggled through the emotional turmoil of repeated infant loss.

Patsy married her high school sweetheart, Scott, when they were twenty and still attending college. Patsy was working toward a teaching degree, but her friends knew the only thing she really wanted to be was a mother.

"I had big plans for five children in five years," says Patsy. "Things did not work out as I had planned."

Patsy did give birth to five children over the next six years, but the experience was far from her ideal. When Patsy realized there was no movement during the twenty-eighth week of her first pregnancy, she and Scott made a medical appointment.

"The doctors tried again and again to find a heartbeat, but there was nothing," says Patsy. "We were so naïve; we had no idea that this type of thing happened. When the nurse walked out, wiping away tears, it finally hit me that the life of our precious baby was gone."

Patsy struggled to deal with the subsequent labor and delivery. In the pre-natal class the couple had taken earlier, the instructor had said, "No matter how much labor pain you experience, the reward will be worth it."

Patsy says, "Those words kept echoing through my mind as I tried to fathom leaving the hospital without my baby."

The couple sought comfort from Scripture and held a funeral service for their son, Daneil, with a message from the first verses of Isaiah 43:

But now thus says the Lord, he who created you . . . he who formed you . . . Fear not, for I have redeemed you; I have called you by name, you are mine . . . Because you are precious in my eyes . . . and I love you . . . Fear not, for I am with you; I will bring your offspring from the east, and from the west I will gather you. I will say to the north, Give up, and to the south, Do not withhold; bring my sons from afar and my daughters from the end of the earth . . . whom I created for my glory, whom I formed and made (vv. 1–7).

An outpouring of compassion from family, church members, and friends demonstrated "true communion of the saints," but Scott and Patsy say their lives "were completely turned around" by their loss. "We were lost for a time," says Scott. "What had been our focus and planning for the last months was suddenly gone, and we had no idea why." Yet they could testify of God's grace: "We were devastated but not in despair."

A few months later, Patsy was again pregnant. She felt as if this was the answer. "Pregnant before Daneil's actual due date," she says, "I thought I had finally found an answer as to *why* Daneil had to die."

But she miscarried at only thirteen weeks. This second grief was compounded by the fact that she had not adequately dealt with the first loss. Since this loss was far earlier in the pregnancy, she and Scott shared this grief with only a few others.

The following year the couple experienced a relatively normal pregnancy that went full term. They were blessed with a healthy son, whom they named Jesse.

Two years later, Scott and Patsy found themselves once more expecting a child. At twenty-four weeks, the baby's movements began to slow. Finally all movement stopped. Baby Ethan died before he was born.

This time the doctors had an explanation. They told Scott and Patsy that all three losses were related to a chromosome problem. The healthy birth of Jesse was described as a "miracle." That explanation and two-year-old Jesse helped them cope. "It was very hard to face another loss," says Patsy, "but having an active two-year-old was sure a good reason to look ahead, not to mention a reason to get out of bed every morning."

Once more a supportive family and church community helped the couple through their sorrow. They found comfort in Psalm 145, which says in part:

> Great is the Lord, and greatly to be praised, and his greatness is unsearchable. One generation shall commend your works to another, and shall declare your mighty acts . . . all your saints shall bless you! They shall speak of the glory of your kingdom and tell of your power, to make known to the children of man your mighty deeds, and the glorious splendor of your kingdom. Your kingdom is an everlasting kingdom, and your dominion endures throughout all generations (vv. 3–4, 10–13).

The following year Patsy experienced a smooth pregnancy until about the seventh month, when movement slowed. She became obsessed with feeling the baby move. She was unable to perform even the simplest activity without first checking for movement. The baby's motion gradually became weaker and weaker. Their daughter, Micah Theresa, died at almost eight months in the womb.

This time the couple turned to Psalm 116, which Patsy had memorized and found to be a "great comfort" during the pregnancy. The Psalm begins, "I love the LORD, because he has heard my voice and my pleas for mercy." The psalmist goes on to describe being "encompassed" by the "snares of death" and suffering "distress and anguish," but resting in the Lord's preservation and deliverance: "Return, O my soul, to your rest; for the LORD has dealt bountifully with you." The Psalm contains that familiar and comforting assurance, "Precious in the sight of the LORD is the death of his saints," and ends with the imperative exclamation: "Praise the LORD!"

"We felt weak, but God was strong; we were shaken, but God was faithful," Patsy says. "God's grace was sufficient." Scott and Patsy again experienced that sufficiency of the Lord's grace through the loving support of fellow believers.

When they realized only a few months later that Patsy was once more pregnant, Scott says they were "shocked and scared." They chose not to share this news with others until almost five months into the pregnancy. Patsy had begun to feel movement, but she didn't want to talk about it. She could barely speak about the pregnancy at all.

"We were pregnant, but not 'expecting,'" she says. "We feared the outcome."

The fear became so intense Patsy became nauseated whenever she performed even ordinary activity. She obsessed about the baby's movement. Before she swept the floor or dressed her son, she forced herself to check if the baby was still moving.

In God's provision, however, the baby was a strong kicker. The couple relates how God "heard and answered" their "many cries to Him." Patsy's pregnancy reached full term. Two weeks after his due date, a healthy and active baby Aaron was born. Since Aaron's birth, the family has adopted Karinna, a "precious" daughter and a younger sister for Jesse and Aaron. "Throughout our trials the Lord was faithful," says Scott. "He blessed us tremendously and increased our faith. We had a lot of questions, but we realize that some will remain unanswered for the rest of our lives."

The family continues to trust God's faithfulness as they raise their children in the Lord. They also continue to remember their children who are already with the Lord. "We visit the little graves at the cemetery occasionally," they say, "just to show our children a bit of their history and to remind them and ourselves of God's covenant faithfulness."

6: Medical Dilemma

Believing parents can take refuge in God's covenant faithfulness, but even believers may struggle with making decisions related to medical treatment.

It was an exciting time for Jeff and Karen. Shortly after Jeff began ministering to his first congregation, they discovered that Karen was pregnant. The couple's excitement doubled when their doctor told them Karen might be carrying twins. Karen was admitted to the hospital with complications, however, in her twelfth week of pregnancy. An ultrasound confirmed the presence of twins, but also indicated that the water sac for one of the twins had broken. That twin was struggling to survive. "This leaves the other twin (and the mother) in a precarious situation," explains Karen. "If the twin who is struggling dies, there is a great risk of infection for both the living twin and the mother."

The couple had intentionally chosen a Christian doctor, hoping he would help guide them through difficult decisions that might arise in a problem pregnancy. The doctor's advice, however, was not what they expected.

"He told me to go home, miscarry both twins, and start over," Karen says. He casually offered to have a visiting specialist give a second opinion. That specialist echoed the first doctor, adding that if the couple really wanted to continue the pregnancy, he would need to treat Karen at a larger hospital.

"So what do you do when you are in an emotional upheaval, you need medical advice, but you don't trust the advice you are getting, as they obviously have no understanding of the sanctity of life?" asked Karen.

Providentially another doctor told Jeff and Karen that they were not obligated to take the previous doctors' advice or remain under their care. This doctor offered to intervene and arrange for transportation to any hospital of the couple's choice within two hundred miles. Jeff suggested a Roman Catholic hospital near his parents' home. Even though Jeff and Karen were not Roman Catholic, they knew the hospital staff would value human life and felt they could trust the diagnosis and care there.

"Within half an hour, I was strapped into a helicopter and headed to the other hospital," Karen says. "It was one of the most difficult times because Jeff was not allowed to come, and so I left him, knowing that I would arrive at the hospital alone, potentially making decisions on how to proceed—all alone."

When she went into labor on the helicopter, Karen's anxiety intensified and she felt overwhelmed by helplessness and panic. She remembers being carried off, "ranting to anyone who would listen that I wanted them to help save my children." One man finally leaned over her and said, "Calm down, lady. You are in a Catholic hospital now. We'll help you."

Karen spent the next four weeks either in the hospital or at the home of her parents-in-law (twenty miles from the hospital) on full bed rest—not even permitted to sit up for food or drink—in an effort to preserve the lives of both children. Jeff made the two-hundred-mile trek weekly, trying to balance his family and ministry commitments.

"To make matters worse, my own mother was recovering from chemotherapy and radiation treatment," Karen says. "We would cry together on the phone, as we both felt guilty that we were not strong enough to help each other." Since Jeff was not always present, Karen was often forced to make difficult medical decisions about treatment for the twins and her own care.

"Any decision regarding one twin affects the other," she says, "and extreme pain can cause the body to go into labor, so each treatment had its pros and cons. It took a lot of trust that the Lord was guiding the doctors to advise what was best."

At sixteen weeks, Karen's complications worsened and she was again admitted to the hospital. Within a week, one of the babies died. "With the loss of the one twin, I experienced more blood loss than the doctors realized," Karen says. "A day later, my blood pressure hit rock bottom and my pulse soared. They thought I had a blood clot in my lung—a potentially fatal situation. The focus went away from the surviving baby in the womb and toward saving me." Karen spent another week in the hospital undergoing various procedures while medical personnel struggled to stabilize her and then the surviving twin.

"One thing we quickly became aware of," Karen says, "is that we should be careful when questioning the decisions that others make in these difficult situations. On the outside, it can seem so clear to us, when in reality the decision is not so easy." Doctors gave the second twin only a ten percent chance of surviving until the twenty-fourth week, when a baby is considered likely to survive outside the womb.

After being released from the hospital, Karen continued on complete bed rest at the home of Jeff's parents. Jeff and Karen did most of their initial grieving for their lost infant while they were apart—"not the way either one of us would have wanted it," they say—describing the time as one of "great emotional confusion."

When the pregnancy reached the twenty-fourth week, Jeff and Karen found themselves confronting a new dilemma. They were told that a baby born between twenty-four and twenty-eight weeks was likely to have enormous health complications and that life-saving techniques would be very painful for the child. If the surviving twin was born during that four-week window, they would have to decide whether or not to initiate life-saving measures that might cause the baby intense suffering.

"It was excruciating to think about, as it was impossible to sort out what was the right answer," Karen says. "Would we be trying to save this little child because it was the right thing to do, or because we wanted the child so much for ourselves? Is there a time when the right thing to do is be merciful and not allow the child to endure so much suffering and be able to go directly to the Father?"

"We never did come to a satisfactory answer," she says. "I woke up every morning of those four weeks and prayed, 'Lord, not today. Give the baby one more day to grow, and give us one more day to decide what to do.'"

In God's providence, Karen's pregnancy lasted past the twenty-eighth week, and the couple was spared from making that difficult decision.

The pregnancy went into its thirtieth week. After "much begging and pleading," Karen was finally permitted to return to her own home, although she remained on partial bed rest. She and Jeff still sorrowed but became more hopeful as Karen's pregnancy continued.

"While we grieved over the loss of our first child," says Karen, "there was also increasing hope about the second." A "completely healthy" baby was born full term. They named him, Josiah, which means "Jehovah heals."

Although they were already mature Christians, Jeff and Karen learned a great deal about total dependence upon the Lord during their difficult dilemmas. Karen admits, "There were times when I felt my cup of endurance was full, and I would cry out, 'Lord, I can't handle any more!' These were the times when the Lord sent one more complication, one more decision about a risky test the doctors wanted to run. Even when we feel like we are on the brink of despair, our Lord is gracious and sustains us. He truly doesn't give us more than we can bear, and He knows what that point is better than we do ourselves. In fact, He often stretches us exactly where we think we can't be stretched, just to show us that we must put our trust solely in Him rather than analyzing for ourselves what is best." Facing difficult medical dilemmas stretched Jeff and Karen's faith and forced them to increasingly depend on the Lord.

7: Hopeless Labor

A pregnancy complicated with medical dilemmas and characterized by difficult decisions can help parents learn total dependence on the Lord. But a sudden loss can also force parents to lean on God's sustaining arms. Infant loss can occur when one least expects it, as it did for Brad and Stephanie.

Brad and Stephanie were eagerly anticipating the arrival of Caleb, who would be only fifteen months younger than their son, Joshua. They envisioned their two sons as happy playmates and planned to homeschool the two boys together. The day before a scheduled induction, baby Caleb was so active during a monitoring session that the technician doubted the doctor would allow Stephanie to go home. The doctor, however, described everything as "textbook perfect" and sent Stephanie home for a good night's rest. When she and Brad arrived at the hospital the next morning, they were shocked to learn there was no heartbeat.

"I was in total disbelief, very confused, and almost immediately became enveloped in a mind-numbing fog," says Stephanie. "Only eighteen hours earlier I had been in my doctor's office, listening to Caleb's heartbeat pounding away for thirty minutes in a non-stress test. And now Caleb was gone? A big part of me was just not going to believe it until I saw him with my own eyes."

Options were to go home and wait for labor to begin naturally, which Stephanie describes as "absolutely unthinkable to me, then and now," or to go ahead with the induction as planned. Stephanie initially insisted on a C-section, but was finally convinced it would entail more risks. "I viewed it as the easy way out," she says. "I think a part of me thought if we could get him out quickly, maybe we could revive him."

When Stephanie realized she would have to go through labor and delivery, she felt far too weak to face the ordeal. Brad reassured her that he would be with her, which he was for the entire fourteen-hour period, reading Scriptures such as 1 Corinthians 15 and Psalm 23 to Stephanie during her lucid moments. "At Caleb's delivery, I remember holding him and crying. He was wrapped in a blanket and beautiful beyond description," says Stephanie, "I felt as if my heart was being ripped out of my chest."

Brad says, "Our dreams that had grown for nine months were shattered."

The nurse assigned to work with the family had experience with stillbirth. She helped Brad bathe Caleb and dress him in a crocheted sweater and hat a woman had donated to the hospital for such situations. She took pictures of Caleb in different poses. "She treated him with the utmost respect," says Stephanie. "She was a wonderful nurse! She stayed past her shift time to be with me; she cried with us." As the couple's parents and Joshua arrived, they took pictures of each family member with Caleb. "We looked at his perfectly formed fingers and toes, his chubby legs, his long lashes," says Stephanie, "his tiny face that looked so much like his brother."

Late in the day, the family needed to move from the delivery room into a private room that was not in the maternity unit. Caleb could not come with them. "I could not bear to have him taken away, as strange as it may sound," says Stephanie. Sensing her distress, the nurses offered to keep Caleb overnight. Brad squeezed into the hospital bed with Stephanie and stayed with her that night. The next day they asked to see Caleb before they left for home. "We held him; his body was very cold and much more discolored than the previous day," she says. "It was wonderful to see him and absolutely horrible at the same time. Finally we kissed his cold blonde head for the last time and left the hospital." As Stephanie was being wheeled out the hospital door, they met a man entering. He was a beaming father carrying blue "Congratulations on your Baby" balloons.

After the funeral, the couple struggled with expectations to get on with life. "I struggled with the everyday tasks of living," says Stephanie. "I struggled just to go to the grocery store and buy only one size of diapers and not two."

The couple also struggled with the medical reason for Caleb's death. An autopsy revealed a healthy baby with no physical defects. This made no sense to them. And the couple struggled with the spiritual reason for Caleb's death. Initially Stephanie questioned God's love. "We had prayed for a healthy baby," says Stephanie, "why had God chosen to answer us with a dead baby?"

Eventually she was able to see demonstrations of God's love. "He displayed so much care for us in the time following Caleb's death," she says, "that I can't even think that anymore!" One way God demonstrated His love was in motivating people from their church family and community to reach out to them. "Many let us know that we were in their prayers," says Brad. "Even some people we did not personally know would speak to Stephanie in public and let her know that they were praying for our family."

Having an active toddler at home was a mixed blessing for Stephanie. She says, "Joshua was both my biggest source of comfort and one of my most agonizing reminders of all that we had lost in losing Caleb." Caring for Joshua helped Stephanie fill her days and find her way through the fog of grief, but it took some time before Stephanie found comfort even in reading the Bible. "I wish I could say that prayer and the Bible brought me great comfort, but in the weeks immediately after Caleb's death, prayer and Bible reading were extremely difficult," she admits. "It was months before the truths of Scripture could penetrate the numbness and fog that had enveloped my heart and mind."

Stephanie recognizes that there previously were areas of immaturity in her faith and now is able to thank God for Caleb's life, even though she still has questions. "I am glad to be working through the tough issues, but I am far from having all the answers," she says. Stephanie found it helpful to focus on Caleb as being in the presence of God "enjoying unimaginable splendor." She was thankful he would never experience the heartbreak of sin. From his conception, she and Brad had prayed that he would know Christ, and she found comfort in acknowledging this as Christ's answer to that prayer. "There is peace in knowing that Caleb is safe, that God is taking infinitely better care of him than I ever could," she says. "Though we never knew our baby, it is assuring to know that he was and is known by God."

"Our God is sovereign over every heartbeat and every breath we take in life," says Brad. "We somehow must rest in His sovereign disposal of all things to the end of His glory. If we do not ultimately find our rest in Him, we will end up hopeless."

8: Father's Love

Those who hope in God are devastated—but not hopeless—when facing infant loss. Even mothers who endure hours of heartrending labor—knowing the finally delivered baby will not be alive—find themselves sustained by God's grace. Over time they are comforted by God's people and calmed by His Word. They see the Father's love in their lives. And God equips grieving fathers to mirror that fatherly love.

Even though they knew they would be busy parents, Mark and Sandi eagerly anticipated the birth of their second child, who would be only a year and a half younger than their son, Andrew. Their anticipation grew as the baby grew in a normal pregnancy.

A week before the baby's due date, Sandi went to the clinic for her scheduled appointment. When the doctor couldn't find a heartbeat, he sent her for monitoring. When he looked at what the monitor was reading, he sent her for an ultrasound. "Nothing was said during the ultrasound," says Sandi. She was sent back to the monitoring room to wait. A short time later, the doctor came in and told her that the baby had died; there was no heartbeat on the ultrasound. "My first reaction was one of shock," says Sandi. "I couldn't believe this had happened. Everything in the pregnancy was going so well. I couldn't understand why this was happening and why to us."

Since this was to have been a regular appointment, Mark had not gone with Sandi and was at work in a town about thirty minutes from the hospital. "I was called out of a meeting and asked to take a call from the hospital," says Mark, "which indicated to me that either unexpectedly she had a baby or otherwise something was wrong."

"When I heard her crying voice it was pretty obvious the news wasn't good," he adds. "When she told me we lost Collin, I left for the hospital, but the emotion didn't really sink in until I held her in my arms."

After Mark and Sandi had some time alone, their doctor came into the room and explained their options. He suggested inducing labor as soon as they were ready. "I was scared and didn't want to go through the labor and delivery knowing the outcome," says Sandi. "Our doctor was very compassionate and understanding and explained things to us very well. He prayed with us, which was very comforting."

The nurses who assisted the couple were also compassionate and supportive through the entire experience. During the early stages of labor, members of their immediate families came to weep with them and express their love and support. As the hours of labor wore on, Mark realized how little he could do for Sandi. "My feelings were mostly of helplessness," he says. "I could tell that this labor experience was extremely tough on my wife and there was nothing that I could do other than to be there for her." In the wee hours of the morning, Sandi's difficult labor finally ended, and a baby boy was delivered. The couple named him Collin James. They held him as they grieved privately together. Overwhelmed by his own grief, Mark says, "I felt torn in that there was no way I could take my wife's grief away."

Soon after Collin's birth, Mark called immediate family members and his pastor, telling them, "The Lord has blessed us with a son." They came to the hospital to share Mark and Sandi's sorrow. "At 3:00 in the morning," says Sandi, "they were there to help us through this difficult journey. What love of a Christian family!"

Sandi was given the option of moving to another part of the hospital, but chose to remain in the OB department for her stay. "My hospital stay was amazingly comforting," she says. "I had such a wonderful doctor and exceptional nurses who were sensitive to our situation and were Christians. It was so nice that our doctor prayed with us, that the nurses told us we were in their prayers. We had never met these nurses before, yet they included us in their prayer life." The couple didn't speak to any friends during their time in the hospital, but Sandi's mother had called their friends to let them know about the loss. She relayed to Mark and Sandi the many expressions of love and assurances of prayer.

On Sunday morning, Mark and Sandi listened to their church's worship service on a radio in the hospital room. They were amazed to hear the title of the sermon: "Collin James, A Congregation in Mourning." "It was a very difficult service to listen to," says Sandi, "yet it brought healing to our hearts even though it had been only a day after Collin's death. To hear the sermon title was so uplifting to us, that not only we were mourning the loss of our son, but the entire congregation was mourning the loss of this child."

Sandi's parents later related to the couple how many people shed tears while listening to the message. "That showed us the bond that exists between Christians during not only the good, but also the bad times," says Sandi. "The love our church family poured out to us was almost overwhelming. To know that we had the support of our church family was a wonderful feeling."

The couple discussed with their parents how the funeral service should be handled. Sandi's father assured them, "You can't do it the wrong way." They decided on a small, private service at a funeral home with about twenty-five family members attending. Using Romans 8:28 as his text, the minister assured the family that God works for the good of those who love Him and are called according to His purpose. The mourners sang, "Children of the Heavenly Father."

After the service, Mark carried Collin's casket to the hearse. At the cemetery, he carried it from the hearse to the gravesite. "That was one of the hardest things to do and watch," says Sandi. "It doesn't seem right for one to carry his son to his grave. Even though we know that Collin is with the Lord, leaving his body at his grave was one of the most difficult things I have ever had to do."

"As Collin's earthly father," Mark says, "I wanted to be the one who gently rested his body on the ground for the final time."

"Although this was tough emotionally, there was a certain amount of closure and fulfillment that I felt by being able to care for my son in this way," he adds. "I believe that is part of my calling as a father, to care for my children from the moment they are conceived to the time that they no longer walk the paths of this earth."

God the Father gave up His one and only Son. He knows the pain that fathers as well as mothers feel in loss. The Father's grace enabled this father to carry out his calling as a father by carrying his infant son to his final resting place.

9: Delivery Distress

God, who willingly gave His only Son for our salvation, knows the pain of loss. He comforts the grieving by using His people to demonstrate His fatherly love. He upholds mothers and fathers through hours of labor when they know the hopeless result. And he upholds mothers and fathers whose expectant labor results in unexpected sorrow.

Randy and Lori had one son, but they longed for another child. After nearly three years and several visits to a specialist, they were overjoyed to discover that—as they say—"we were pregnant." When they told four-year-old Matthew about his anticipated sibling, he was delighted, too. They told him, "This is our secret for a while." Those first few weeks, when just the three of them knew and talked about the baby, were precious. When they gave Matthew permission to tell his grandparents, he couldn't help himself—he told everyone he met. Store clerks, grocery carryouts, and bank tellers soon all knew the family's good news.

Lori's first contraction came late one night as she was preparing for bed. The contractions soon became stronger and closer together. Randy called Lori's mother to care for Matthew and he and Lori were at the hospital by midnight. As Lori's labor grew more intense, she requested pain medication. When the nurse told her that she first had to find a good heartbeat with the monitor, Lori assumed she meant that she couldn't find a good spot because of the baby's movement.

When the doctor arrived, he asked some questions and didn't like what he saw on the heartbeat strip, so he used a scalp electrode for another reading. "This one must be defective," he said, "get me another one."

"He placed another one," says Lori, "and I knew something wasn't right."

The doctor said, "We need to deliver this baby as soon as possible." He called for an emergency C-section "stat," but by 1:50 a.m. the baby's heartbeat was very slow.

"Things got very hectic with people in and out," says Lori. She quickly dilated far enough that the doctor told her to start pushing. "I pushed as hard and as fast as I could," says Lori. The baby was born at 2:00 a.m. and immediately taken to a portable crib in the room. Two more doctors came in. Lori recalls the blur of activity following the baby's delivery: "I remember asking, 'Is it a boy or a girl?' It was a girl, Sarah Renee. I remember hearing the doctors talking and working on her. I remember Randy saying, 'Come on, Sarah,' at my head. I remember nurses coming to me and saying, 'They are doing everything they can.' I remember a nurse cleaning me up a bit. Most of all, I remember praying for all I was worth, 'Please, God. Please.' Then, 'Thy will be done.'"

After forty-five minutes, Lori's doctor came to her side and said he was sorry, that they had tried everything, but the baby died. Randy cried. Lori's first reaction was fear. "I was terrified they would immediately take the baby away," she says. Lori asked the doctor if she could hold her. "He wrapped her up and handed her to me," she says. "He took some pictures for us and told us we would have as much time as we wanted with her."

Sometime during the night in the delivery room, Lori remembers the doctor saying, "The Lord giveth, the Lord taketh away; Blessed be the name of the Lord." Randy and Lori asked if other family members would be permitted to come to the hospital and see the baby. When the doctor assured them they could, Lori asked if Sarah could be cleaned up a bit first. While the doctor finished working with Lori, she watched a nurse bathe Sarah. "I cried the entire time," Lori says. "The nurse was so gentle and loving. She dressed Sarah in the outfit we brought to take her home in. She cut a lock of her hair for us and took footprints. When she was finished, she handed her to me. I remember thinking, 'She will breathe any minute.'"

Grandparents, other relatives, their church elder, and their pastor all arrived early that Sunday morning. Anyone who wanted to hold Sarah was given the opportunity. Lori and Randy felt it was best if Matthew wasn't present during this time of intense grief.

The couple asked the pastor to make an announcement at that morning's worship service. Randy then called other friends and family to let them know about Sarah's death before they heard the announcement at church.

After discussing it with their parents and pastor, the couple decided on a funeral service at their church. They worked through a myriad of details with the funeral director. "There are so many aspects we had never considered before," Lori said. "Things like day and time, visitation, songs, caskets, and burial plots."

"From the time she was delivered, we had six short hours with her," Lori says. "After the funeral director left with her, I felt empty." Within an hour after Sarah's departure, Lori was moved from the OB department to a regular hospital room. She credits hospital personnel with "much sensitivity." The couple requested a radio so they could listen to the church service. As they listened, they were "surprised and strengthened" by an entire worship service that had been adjusted to fit their situation.

When Matthew arrived at the hospital, they tried to explain Sarah's death to him, but he didn't seem to understand. He was more interested in all the visitors. That night Randy went home and put all the furniture, equipment, toys, and clothing the couple had prepared for Sarah into one room and shut the door.

Lori went home the next day. Although they had many visitors, the only thing she remembers from that day is the conversation with Matthew over the evening meal. "We explained to him that his sister—whom we had spent so much time talking about—had died," Lori says. "That when she was born, she couldn't breathe, and that she was gone from us, but alive in heaven."

After a while, Matthew said, "Next time I hope we have a boy, because I was a boy and I breathed." Randy and Lori reminded him of other baby girls he knew, realizing that in spite of this misconception, he still understood something of what they'd told him. Matthew told his parents that he wished he could have seen her. They showed him pictures of Sarah, and told him he would see her at the visitation.

Visitation was difficult for the family. It was the first time Matthew saw Sarah and the first time that Randy and Lori had seen her since the hospital. "She looked beautiful," Lori says. "She had on her white dress and her fingernails had been carefully coated with a pale pink polish."

There were many, many visitors; most of whom tightly hugged Lori. "By that time my milk had come in and I was very uncomfortable," Lori says, "but even though I was uncomfortable, I wasn't going to turn down a hug."

The funeral was the next day. Lori recalls telling her mother, "I'm not sure I can do this." Her mother replied, "We have to; God will get us through it." The couple chose Job 1:21 as the text for the funeral, which was the same verse quoted by their doctor in the delivery room: "The LORD gave, and the LORD has taken away; Blessed be the name of the LORD" (NKJV). The pastor read the first question and answer from the Heidelberg Catechism and Article I/17 from the Canons of Dort. Lori reflects, "One moment that stands out in my memory is our pastor saying, 'Lori, you are the mother of two children: one is here on earth, and one is in heaven.'"

Part Three: Bearing Infertility's Loss

10: Empty Womb

Infant loss is not always as obvious as a dramatic loss during delivery. Loss can be a painful and continual condition. Greg and Bonnie had been married for about four years when they began trying to have a baby. They became increasingly concerned when they didn't conceive, but they were elated two years later when Bonnie finally became pregnant. "We were ecstatic!" they say. "We were so very happy and relieved that the long wait was finally over." Eager to share their long-awaited joy, they told all their family and friends the good news. But three days before Christmas, Bonnie miscarried at about ten weeks. Greg and Bonnie were both distraught. Bonnie plunged into utter despair and could not be comforted. She spent several days in bed, sobbing uncontrollably.

"One of the hardest parts was that I felt as if others just couldn't understand the depths of my grief," she says. "After all, I hadn't really lost a child, at least in their minds. But in my heart and soul I *knew* I had lost a child." It was difficult to tell others about the loss. It was difficult for them to know how to respond. And it was difficult for Bonnie to hear things like, "Don't worry, you'll get pregnant again," or, "It's all in God's hands."

But Bonnie did not get pregnant again. "The feeling of loss grew over the years into an even greater longing for a child," she says. "Year after year, procedure after procedure, it appeared that the incessant struggle with painful medical conditions and surgeries would not allow the ever-increasing desire for a child to be realized. The cavern of loss grew deeper every year."

The couple's pain intensified as more and more of their friends had children. "The more joyous our friends were," they say, "the more deeply the knife cut into our own soul of grief." The couple felt guilty about their lack of joy for their friends with children and also felt an increasing sense of isolation from them. Attending worship services was painful, especially for Bonnie, who struggled to hold back tears as she saw all the children God had provided for others in their age group, but not for Greg and her.

"Year after year, sorrow upon sorrow, we finally came to the realization that I would probably never conceive," Bonnie says. "My womb would never be satisfied. As Proverbs 30:16 says, the barren woman is never satisfied. The exhausting pursuit for a child had become a strenuous road to walk." Now in her mid-forties, Bonnie mourns the loss of opportunity to have a child in her lifetime. The death of anticipation for a baby in her womb is a constant loss. "There will not be a dreamed-for baby," she says, "All the babies I ever dreamed about having will never be realized."

The fear of additional loss, the lack of emotional energy, and the huge financial toll kept the couple from actively pursuing adoption. But mourning constant loss isn't the end of the story for Greg and Bonnie. "Over this fifteen year period of loss, we have learned not only to cope, but we have also grown and actually flourished because of God's gracious blessing in our lives." Bonnie adds, "I'm not sure I can say there is an end to the life of loss. I can't say that the feeling of loss and the feeling of mourning the death of a child and the death of any hope of having a child will ever be completely gone. It stays with me all the time. But God's marvelous grace and love and compassion and joy shine through me even brighter. Perhaps the greater the sadness, the deeper the cavern of loss, the stronger God's love burns through that loss and refines us more thoroughly to glorify Him."

In contrast to many mothers who do not have time or energy to pursue creative outlets, Bonnie is a talented photographer with her own business. She copes with her grief by utilizing her gift. "Since I am able to do something I absolutely love to do every single work day of my life, it helps to lessen the ache I have for children," she says. "God's amazing beauty in nature has given me great comfort in this life. It salves my soul and calms my fear when I can take pieces of the puzzle (light, expression, color, movement, perspective, composition) and create a work of art with my camera. It comforts me in the most fulfilling way imaginable. It gives me the greatest joy! It relieves the pain of living in a fallen world, with all its heartbreak, even if just for a moment. I am so thankful to have been given the gift to create and the courage to do it. It's God's 'bundle of joy' to me."

Greg creates beautiful spaces for people through his gifts for design and finish carpentry. The couple lives in an apartment he renovated in the barn on their farm. They enjoy caring for goats and chickens as well as renting the farmhouse as a vacation retreat for couples or families. They also practice hospitality within their church and minister to the needy. This lifestyle of caring helps lessen the pain of childlessness. "We love being able to be hospitable with our wonderful farm," they say. "It gives us great joy to share it with others."

They recommend keeping busy when in a long-term mourning process. "Keeping my brain busy in a creative way has truly helped keep me from any extreme psychological distress," Bonnie says. "Doing what I *love* to do for work, and not just what pays the bills, has helped me to maintain overall mental wellness."

Another gift that has helped the couple cope is the privilege of being asked to care for children should their parents die. Greg and Bonnie are designated guardians for ten children in four different families. "We definitely wouldn't want all of the parents flying on the same plane," they say. "But we know God would provide if anything should happen to all the parents. We have four empty bedrooms at our farmhouse." In addition to these children, Greg and Bonnie have many nieces and nephews and a host of other children who call them "Uncle Greg" and "Aunt Bonnie." They say, "It gives us a thrill every time we hear it and every time they come running up for hugs."

Some friends faithfully invite them to their children's birthday parties each year. The attention and love of these children help calm any fears Greg and Bonnie might have when they think about their aging years. "God provides in His own way in His own timing," they say. "We can trust Him for our future needs."

Greg and Bonnie have not ruled out the possibility of fostering or adopting children. They sometimes dream of filling the farmhouse with up to a dozen needy children who would grow to honor and glorify God. "Praise be to God if it happens! Praise be to God if it doesn't!" they say. "We know that our lives are fragile but that they are in His hands. He will mold and shape our lives as He wishes. We have learned to be content, whatever our circumstances. We have been blessed with the gift of our Lord Jesus Christ. We do not need a full womb to be satisfied; we really need Christ! He turns our mourning into dancing! Praise be to God in want or in plenty!"

11: Childless Marriage

Loss can be a chronic condition following a miscarriage or it can be the chronic ache of infertility—without even the briefest pregnancy or a miscarriage, but with a series of losses that are not easily labeled. When Russ and Amanda met, they knew that God had brought them into each other's lives. They weren't focused on having a family; they just wanted to be married. After four and half years of marriage, the couple decided to try to have children. About a year later, Amanda's doctor suggested tests. The couple discussed how far they were willing to go in the infertility treatment process. They discovered a shared willingness to proceed with early steps as well as a shared reluctance to go as far as *in vitro fertilization* (IVF).

"I was still hopeful that some of the earlier steps would be enough to result in a successful pregnancy," Amanda says. "We knew that, whatever happened, God had a plan for our lives together, and we knew that His plan was perfect."

"I think," says Russ, "we were trying to find the balance between 'leaving things up to God' (perhaps kids are not part of His plan for us) and 'using the things God has given us' (perhaps we should try some of the medical intervention stuff). IVF seemed like a *lot* of human involvement in God's established process of conception."

Additional considerations were IVF's prohibitive cost (not covered by insurance) and Amanda's unwillingness to subject her body to an unnatural process. They had seen other couples experience the emotional turmoil of failed cycles and miscarriages with IVF and were reluctant to spend thousands of dollars only to experience heartache while testing the limits of their emotional and physical health.

But even the first steps of infertility treatments were an emotional roller coaster. "The emotional ups and downs were devastating," says Amanda. "Infertility completely takes over every part of your life."

Through the agonizing three-year process, the couple never saw a positive pregnancy test. An emotionally drained Amanda watched friends who easily became pregnant "over and over again." She felt isolated when conversations with friends were dominated by topics such as pregnancy, breast feeding, and potty training. "Their lives revolved around nap times and play dates, and mine stayed stagnantly the same."

Attending church was the most difficult part of her week. There she was surrounded by families, heard messages about passing one's faith on to one's children, and watched baptisms week after week. But the worst thing was the frequent question, "When are you going to have kids?" Russ recalls suggesting at one point that they answer that with, "When are you going to lose weight?"

"Just once," Amanda says, "I wish I would have answered that question with the honest ugly truth of all we were doing to try to achieve parenthood. Yet, by the grace of God, I made it through those dark hours and came out a more compassionate person."

The darkest hour was the point when the couple walked away from treatments. "That was a very hard day," says Amanda. "The hardest part was the finality of it. There was no 'one more thing to try.' Being childless was going to affect us for the rest of our lives. I've been told that it's like learning you have a terminal illness. It changes how you make lifelong decisions—where you live, what car you drive, whom you leave your belongings to when you die—and this finality happens in a matter of seconds."

"It did seem like a very 'final' thing in many ways," Russ adds. "I think there was a definite sense of loss—of the parenting experience, of our cool kid that might have been, and of the commonality between friends. But it was the start of us growing stronger as we dealt with it together."

"With infertility comes loss," says Amanda. "It is a guaranteed combination! During the years of trying to conceive there is a great loss of control. When that ends, other losses creep in: the loss of never experiencing pregnancy, the loss of never knowing what our biological child would look like or act like (would we have a boy or girl, with my nose or his lips, outgoing like me or smart like him?);

so many never-knows. The loss is not mine alone. It extends to my parents and siblings. My parents now experience the loss of never being grandparents, and my brother will never be an uncle. This has been an unexpected and hard loss to accept."

Walking away from further treatment was a difficult day, and the couple continues to have other days that are hard. "Hard days come in two forms for me," says Amanda. "First, days when my peers endlessly complain about how difficult it is to be a parent, how their kids never sleep, are so expensive, are always sick, and control their entire lives. It upsets me to hear people complain about how something they wanted and easily received makes them unhappy when there is effort involved on their part. (News flash! It's called being a good parent!)"

"Second, hard days come when I feel isolated from the world around me," she adds. "Our society has a fascination with 'parenting.' In every aisle of the grocery store, there is some child-centered product: diapers, baby Tylenol, juice boxes, and chicken soup with ABC noodles! When you don't have children, the world can be a very lonely place."

By God's grace, Russ and Amanda remarkably accept their childless state as God's will. They focus on modeling a great marriage. "God has given us a very generous dose of grace and peace," they say. "Our marriage has always been our first priority, and we feel so blessed to have such an amazing marriage."

Russ and Amanda have discussed adoption but have not felt led to it. "Adoption is a big deal," they say. "It's expensive, it's parenting to the extreme, and it doesn't replace the child you couldn't have together. It's not a quick fix for childlessness. It's a decision that needs to be bathed in prayer and properly thought out. As of right now, God has not put that desire in our hearts. Maybe someday He will, but until then, we are fully content in our childless state."

Russ and Amanda realize that having no children allows them more opportunities for ministering to others. Amanda can be "flexible and spontaneous" in her work with church youth. She attends their sports events and school plays; she spends weeks with them on summer mission trips. Russ participates in an improvisation team; he finds it easier to travel for his frequent "improv hobby" commitments without children at home.

Russ copes by focusing on these positive aspects of not having children and showing others that it is still possible to have a great marriage. "I've always found it easy to trust God, and I've lived through some other low times," he says, "so 'giving it up' to Him is a burden released in many ways."

"My main coping strategy," Amanda says, "is reading God's Word and finding my perfect identity in Him. I love reading Hebrews 11 and 12 after a hard day. Hebrews 11 is all about the faith of those who have gone before us, who did not receive the things promised but only saw them from a distance. The line of faithful believers continues."

"Providence and God's plan have always played a big part in each of our lives and our life together," they say, "and knowing God's ultimately in control is what continues to comfort and sustain us."

12: Supernatural Children

Although some infertile couples are led to accept their childless state as God's will for their lives, others feel compelled to pursue the adoption option. Since biological children are known as *natural* children, it makes perfect sense that Brian and Sally call their four adopted children their *supernatural* children. "Any descriptor that falls short of *natural* seems somehow *less*," says Sally, "but I perceive my children as so much *more* that *supernatural* seems to fit them and their providential placement into our family."

After years of trying to have children, Brian and Sally consulted an infertility specialist. The couple continued treatments during Brian's pastoral internship but eventually decided to pursue adoption rather than treatment. To avoid the expense and time involved in private adoptions, they chose to adopt through the state. Because children are available for adoption only after at least a year—often several years— in foster care, they opted for a dual license: foster care/adoption. "This would allow us to be the first home a child entered when removed from the family," they explain. "We knew that we ran the risk of losing a child, but at least we would be able to parent right away."

Unfortunately, "right away" took nearly two and a half years. But only a week after they finally obtained their license, God's amazing providence became apparent. As a pastor and wife, Brian and Sally often invited regular church visitors to their home for meals. One couple had begged off several invitations, but Brian called Sally one day to suggest inviting them again. Sally thought Brian wasn't getting the hint and felt they should leave the couple alone, but Brian was persistent, and Sally relented. Once more the couple had an excuse. The wife explained that her husband, a Department of Human Services (DHS) employee, was on call with a case that weekend. Brian mentioned that he and Sally had finally received their DHS foster care license and were hoping to adopt. Although this couple had been attending Brian's church for several months, the woman had not been aware of Brian and Sally's efforts.

A few hours later, the husband came to Brian and Sally's home. He told them he expected to take custody of a baby directly from the hospital that weekend and asked, "Would you like to have the child placed with you?" After more than two years of waiting for their license and nearly seven years of marriage, Brian and Sally were thrilled at the prospect of caring for a child—and amazed at the rare opportunity to receive a newborn.

That same night, they learned the mother was in labor. They chose the name Matthew (gift of the Lord) David (beloved). After a nearly sleepless night, they received a call the next morning informing them that the baby had been born only two hours earlier. Because they did not live in the same county as the child, they needed special permission to be his foster parents in a pre-adoptive placement. In a rare move within the foster system, permission was granted for placement across county lines, since there would be no attempt at family reunification (which was also uncommon). In yet another rarity within the foster care system, Brian and Sally were permitted to visit their son that evening—on the same day he was born. "We held our son at 7:00 p.m.," they say, "and we cried."

The next day was Sunday. After Brian finished leading the worship service, he announced, "You will have to excuse me today. I will not be staying after the service to greet you. I need to go to the hospital to pick up my son."

"There was not a dry eye in the church," Sally says, "Infertile couple—pastor and his wife—waiting for their license for over two years, and to them—a baby was born!"

When Matthew was almost two, the couple took a fifteen-month-old boy for a weekend as respite care for his foster family. Since he had already been in three foster homes, Brian and Sally were asked to consider being his permanent foster placement. "This sweet, happy, strapping toddler boy came walking through our door, and we adopted him two and a half years later," they say. "That is our Michael Henry."

Shortly after Michael's arrival, the couple was contacted about a baby expected to be born in six months. While they waited for that child, they turned down placements for two other babies. Their anticipated child was born on Sunday, and the DHS called on Monday to make sure Brian and Sally were still willing to take him, since he would be discharged from the hospital the next day. On Tuesday, they received a terrible blow: they were told that other arrangements had been made. "I felt like I'd had a miscarriage," Sally says. "I was devastated."

But the very next day, they were asked if they would foster a six-week-old girl. Although they initially thought this little girl would live with them only a short time, Elizabeth Marie officially became their daughter nearly two years later. "Foster care can be stressful," Sally admits. "At one point I had nine standing appointments a week—not including doctor's visits, family meetings, and social worker visits—while caring for a three-, two-, and one-year-old and wondering if they would stay or go."

"Foster parenting gives you a unique perspective," she adds. "None of us actually owns our children; we are all stewards of the children God has placed in our care. But when you foster parent a child, there is an even keener sense of this stewardship responsibility and a deep sense of gratitude for the privilege of parenting."

By the time Brian accepted a call to pastor a church in another state, the couple had adopted three children out of four long-term placements (the fourth child had been reunited with his family after four months). Feeling led to adopt more children, they underwent a six-month licensing and training process in their new state.

Five months later, they were planning a trip that would have put their cell phone in a "no service" zone, but their departure was delayed several hours. When they were finally ready to leave, they received a call asking if they would take a two-month-old boy. They canceled their trip and spent the next hour quickly converting a spare room into a nursery. Two hours later, they came home with a baby boy. A little over a year later, Ian Theodore officially became their son. "Truly God has filled our quiver," Brian says, "even as we approach our mid forties!"

"It's clear to me now that God always intended for us to adopt," says Sally. "The fun part has been those instances when God peeled back the curtain for us to see how He orchestrated events to build our family. As I look back, the infertility part seems like a sidebar in my life. It was a time when God molded me and transformed me from thinking that childbearing was the ultimate blessing into cherishing the blessing of union with Christ. And He did this for me and in me long before He placed a child in my arms. So I have been twice blessed through infertility and adoption, first in my heart and then in my home."

"Understanding God's sovereignty has been important through the process," Brian says. "But God's sovereignty is not simply neutral; a Christian minister told me, 'When a covenant child is born, that's plus one for the kingdom; but when one is adopted, it's plus one for the kingdom—and minus one for Satan!' By God's providence, He has chosen to use us to rescue four children from troubled lives and bring them up within His covenant so that, by His grace and goodness, they might share with us the hope of eternal life through Jesus Christ."

Part Four: Finding Our Comfort

13: Not Lost

Couples who have never had a child may feel the loss as keenly as those who have experienced early infant loss, whether that experience was tranquil or traumatic. Grieving couples may initially identify with the "weeping and great mourning" described as the "voice of Ramah" in Matthew 2. When Herod realized the wise men had no intention of returning to report the location of the newly born "King of the Jews," he was furious. He ordered the deaths of all boys under the age of two in Bethlehem and its surrounding area (v. 16). Echoing Jeremiah's dreadful prophecy (31:15), Matthew records its atrocious fulfillment: "A voice was heard in Ramah, Weeping and great mourning, Rachel weeping for her children; And she would not be comforted, because they are not" (2:18, ASV).

If these Jewish children "are not," have they ceased to exist? Has the essence of their brief existence been annihilated? Are they sleeping in a state of comatose limbo? These children "are not" only in the sense that they are no longer with their parents. Their souls continue to exist in a conscious state between death and the final resurrection. So, too, the littlest ones lost through miscarriage, stillbirth, or newborn death are no longer with their parents, but are not lost. The loss is temporal, not eternal.

The phrase "are not" is similar to Genesis 5:24: "Enoch walked with God, and he was not, for God took him." Enoch "was not" only in the sense that he no longer walked on earth. He walked in fellowship with God during his earthly existence, and he now walks in fellowship with God during his heavenly existence. God took Enoch—soul *and* body—immediately and directly to heaven.

The story of Job clearly demonstrates continued existence after death. Job was a man who had it all: seven thousand sheep, three thousand camels, five hundred yoke of oxen, and five hundred female donkeys. He also had seven sons and three daughters (Job 1:2–3). In a progressively tragic series of events, he loses everything: sheep, camels, oxen, donkeys, and finally his children (1:13–19). God eventually restores Job's fortune, giving him "twice as much as he had before" (42:10). Job then had fourteen thousand sheep, six thousand camels, one thousand yoke of oxen, and one thousand female donkeys (42:12). But God gave him only seven sons and three daughters, which was the same amount as his loss (42:13). God gave Job the same number of children because his original seven sons and three daughters still existed.

The conscious state of souls after death is known as the *intermediate state*. It is called *intermediate* because it is between life in an earthly body and life in a resurrected and glorified body, but the term should not be understood to mean a vague or shadowy existence in some kind of holding pattern. Souls do not strum insipid music on harps while drifting aimlessly on puffy white clouds high in the blue sky. The harp imagery has a biblical basis, but it's quite different from such a popular misconception. John describes his glimpse of heaven as seeing "those who had conquered" standing with harps in their hands beside what "appeared to be a sea of glass mingled with fire" (Rev. 15:2). The image of flames flickering within a glass sea is a far cry from innocuous cumulus clouds! Those holding harps sing rousing praise to God the Almighty that is equally far removed from bland strumming (Rev. 15:3). This stirring picture should dispel any idea of souls floating in limbo. But the intermediate state is not only conscious and active; it is also immediate. Christ told the thief on the cross beside him, "Truly, I say to you, *today* you will be *with me* in *Paradise*" (Luke 23:43, emphasis added). His words leave absolutely no doubt: the believer has instant access to fellowship with Christ in heaven.

The Heidelberg Catechism beautifully ties together the comfort of instant access to Christ with the hope of resurrection through Christ. Question 57 asks, "How does 'the resurrection of the body' comfort you?" The answer is clear: "Not only my soul will be taken immediately after this life to Christ its head, but even my very flesh, raised by the power of Christ, will be reunited with my soul and made like Christ's glorious body." This confession confirms the immediacy of the soul's fellowship with Christ in heaven. It also affirms the guarantee of the soul's reunion with a glorified body. Believers can have good confidence that their little "lost" ones now live with Christ in heaven. One day their souls will reunite with their resurrected bodies and they—with their parents—will enjoy the unimaginable glories of fellowship with God and the Lamb in the new heaven and earth.

About one hundred years before Jeremiah prophesied "weeping and great mourning," Isaiah proclaimed a prophecy that assures believers of the future resurrection. His vivid imagery strikes a responsive chord with grieving parents:

> Your dead shall live; their bodies shall rise.
> You who dwell in the dust, awake and sing for joy!
> For your dew is a dew of light,
> and the earth will give birth to the dead (Isa. 26:19).

Mourners crawling in a grief-induced stupor through this earth's dust will wake from their daze. They can rejoice in God's promise that they will witness the bodies of loved ones waking from sleep in the dust. They then will sing joyfully with their "lost" children. God's sparkling dew of light will water and illuminate the earth's dry and drab dust. The dead will burst forth into life in a resurrection event reminiscent of a joyful birth.

Isaiah also prophesied the comforting verse found in the front of this book:

> He will tend his flock like a shepherd;
> he will gather the lambs in his arms;
> he will carry them in his bosom,
> and gently lead those that are with young (40:11).

The Good Shepherd—not a ravaging wolf or a prowling lion—"gathers" the lambs. He does not seize them from their mothers' sides or rip them from their arms. In His sovereign will, He gathers them to Himself. He does not shut them up in a pen with other bleating lambs; He carries each little one snuggled securely in His arms. He does not leave the mother to find her way alone; He doesn't allow her to fall off a cliff or to plunge into quicksand. He leads her gently and carefully along safe paths. This is a comforting image that parents can carry in their hearts. It will not fill the aching void, but it can begin to blunt the sharpness of its raw and jagged edges.

73

The consoling image of God as the Good Shepherd also is depicted in David's familiar and beloved Psalm 23: "The LORD is my shepherd; I shall not want" (v. 1). God is the Sovereign Shepherd who cares for His sheep through every step of the journey. He provides all they need: food, water, security, guidance, and peace. That peace is possible even when His sheep walk through their own "valley of the shadow of death" or when they stumble through the dark valley of losing a loved one. The Shepherd's "rod and staff" would seem to be sources of painful correction, but David says, "They comfort me" (v. 4). The Great Shepherd guides and comforts His sheep into the ordained paths. The sheep may never understand why they are poked or prodded, why they must walk through arid deserts or stony valleys; but they can know that the Shepherd is directing each step. And He is with them.

Although most parents may initially identify with the emotions of the distraught Bethlehem mothers, who "would not be comforted," believing parents *can* find comfort. Believers can know and trust that God is both sovereign *and* loving. He is almighty God who rules over all the events of life, but He is also our Father and the Great Shepherd of His sheep. He tenderly cares for even the littlest lambs, who may be lost from their parents, but who are known to Him and secure in His arms.

14: Biblical Comfort

Believers can trust their sovereign and loving God to keep the beautiful promises He gives His children in His Word. In all of life's struggles, few verses are as comforting as the marvelous promise of God's sovereignty found in Romans 8:28:

> And we know that all things work together for good to those who love God, to those who are the called according to His purpose (NKJV).

God sovereignly uses even the overwhelming grief of infant loss for His divine purposes. God can use this furnace of affliction like fire that purifies gold. It may be years before we see how God used it for good. Or we may live our entire lives without ever seeing the good or understanding a reason for our suffering. In either case, we can know God's promise is true. We can trust Him to work even this for His good purposes.

Job's story is instructive. God has an extensive dialogue with Job, asking him question after question designed to demonstrate His sovereignty (Job 38–41). But God never tells Job, "Oh, by the way, the reason you're suffering is that Satan thought you'd deny me if I removed my protection from you, so I allowed him to cause pain in your life to show that you would remain righteous." He doesn't even say, "You know, Job, generations of believers will draw immense comfort from your story of suffering." God doesn't explain any kind of reason to Job. God simply and powerfully articulates His sovereignty. Job doesn't learn a reason, but he learns he must trust this sovereign God.

Just as believers can trust God to work all things for our good, we can trust God to work all things for our future glory. In 2 Corinthians 4:17, Paul compares our present suffering to our future glorification:

"For our light and momentary troubles are achieving for us an eternal glory that far outweighs them all" (NIV84). Even the heaviest and most prolonged of our struggles in this life is *light* and *momentary* compared to the substantial weight of our future glory—a glory that, in some way we cannot understand, is being achieved by those very struggles.

The book of Psalms overflows with comfort for believers. God is our refuge and strength, our ever-present help in trouble (Ps. 46:1). He is our rock in whom we take refuge (Ps. 18:2). The Lord is our strength and shield; when our hearts trust in Him, we are helped (Ps. 28:7). When our hearts and minds are so burdened by the loss of a tiny infant that we cannot articulate prayers, we can pray God's own words back to Him. Reflect on this beautiful prayer from Psalm 73: "You guide me with your counsel, and afterward you will receive me to glory. Whom have I in heaven but you? And there is nothing on earth that I desire besides you" (vv. 24–25). God the Holy Spirit comforts us in our struggles and guides us with His counsel. God the Son is our eternal advocate in heaven, and He is all we need on earth. He will take us and our lost infants to glory.

"Give ear to my words, O LORD," the Psalmist writes, "consider my groaning. Give attention to the sound of my cry . . . Lead me, O LORD, in your righteousness" (Ps. 5:1–2, 8a). God hears our inarticulate groans. He listens to our brokenhearted cries. He not only will bring peace to our minds and comfort to our souls but He also will lead us in such a way that we can move forward in righteousness.

Psalm 28 begins with a heartfelt entreaty that can be held in our hearts: "To you, O LORD, I call; my rock, be not deaf to me . . . Hear the voice of my pleas for mercy, when I cry to you for help" (vv. 1–2). This Psalm ends with a prayer evocative of Isaiah 40's shepherd imagery (which appears at the front of this book and was discussed in the previous chapter): "Oh, save your people and bless your heritage! Be their shepherd and carry them forever" (v. 9). This is another heartfelt plea that we can pray to God.

When you feel overwhelmed with sorrow and bowed down with grief over the loss of your little one, you can echo David: "But you, O LORD, are a shield about me, my glory, and the lifter of my head"

(Ps. 3:3). God wraps His shield of comfort and protection around us. Our hope is securely anchored in God's eternal glory, not in the events of this temporal life. When your head hangs in despair, God tucks His hand under your chin and lifts it up in hope.

As we pray the Psalms in our distress, we can cling to the hope of God's Word: "Let your steadfast love, O Lord, be upon us, even as we hope in you" (Ps. 33:22). "You are my hiding place and my shield; I hope in your word" (Ps. 119:114). God's love stands firm through all life's storms and enables us to hope in Him. If we feel like crawling into a hole and dying, we can crawl onto our Father's lap and hide ourselves in the bosom of His protective love. His Word brings us hope.

The hope of God's Word comforts us as we groan in the earthly tents of our weak and deteriorating bodies:

> For we know that if the tent that is our earthly home is destroyed, we have a building from God, a house not made with hands, eternal in the heavens . . . For while we are still in this tent, we groan, being burdened—not that we would be unclothed, but that we would be further clothed, so that what is mortal may be swallowed up by life. He who has prepared us for this very thing is God, who has given us the Spirit as a guarantee. So we are always of good courage. We know that while we are at home in the body we are away from the Lord, for we walk by faith, not by sight (2 Cor. 5:1, 4–7).

Our earthly tent swiftly deteriorates, but we have an eternal home in heaven. We walk through life burdened by physical struggles that weaken our bodies and grief that saps our strength. We groan under our heavy burden, not longing to be rid forever of our bodies, but longing to reside eventually in perfect and glorified bodies. That longing will be beautifully fulfilled when Christ returns and dynamic resurrection swallows up this decrepit tent! God Himself has prepared our eternal home and has given us the Holy Spirit as a guarantee. Because the Holy Spirit guarantees our future, we can be of "good courage." The hope of our future reality enables us to walk toward that home with faith, not becoming bogged down by the appearance of reality we see in this world.

Christ Himself promised this home: "In My Father's house are many rooms; if it were not so, would I have told you that I go to prepare a place for you?" (John 14:2). Christ personally promised a room with your name on the door! Our heavenly home will be free from grief for all eternity. The Lamb who was slain is the Great Shepherd. Christ will guide His people to springs of living water and "will wipe away every tear from their eyes" (Rev. 7:17). Our tears on earth may seem endless, but Christ in heaven will definitively dry them.

When we toss and turn on sleepless nights, our hot pillowcase absorbing our tears, we can remind ourselves of Psalm 56:8, "You have kept count of my tossings; put my tears in your bottle. Are they not in your book?" God chronicles each toss and collects every tear. If my tears can be contained in a bottle, their number is limited. My finite tears are kept by an infinite God. Our earthly tears are only temporary. "Weeping may tarry for the night, but joy comes with the morning" (Psalm 30:5). Christ will bring the dawn of a bright new day. He will resurrect our old bodies and glorify them into new bodies that will never decay or grieve. Our decrepit mortal tents will become vigorous immortal temples.

This remarkable renovation is sure. "For this corruptible *must* put on incorruption, and this mortal *must* put on immortality. So when this corruptible has put on incorruption, and this mortal has put on immortality, then shall be brought to pass the saying that is written: 'Death is swallowed up in victory.' 'O Death, where in your sting? O Hades, where is your victory?'" (1 Cor. 15:53–55, NKJV, emphasis added). This transformation *must* occur! Life will swallow death, conquering and destroying it forever!

15: Covenantal Comfort

Grieving believers are comforted by God's beautiful promises that Christ has overcome death and will bring the dawn of a new day. God's promises mean even more when considered within the context of His covenant with His people. Throughout human history, God has compassionately dealt with His children within the comprehensive scope of His covenant. His relationship with His people is one of covenant faithfulness.

A covenant is a bond of friendship and fellowship. God often compares His relationship with His people to the marriage covenant, which is a promise of faithfulness between a husband and wife. But while His promise to be a God to believers and their children never fails, we frequently fail in our responsibility to love God and obey Him. As our covenant representative and the second Adam, Christ fulfilled our covenantal requirements by living a life of perfect obedience and by giving His life as the perfect payment for our sin. Through His finished work, His church becomes His perfect bride.

The concept of covenant permeates Scripture; it is a primary theme that runs throughout the entire Bible. Already in Genesis, God promised to be with Abraham and his descendants: "And I will establish my covenant between me and you and your offspring after you throughout their generations for an everlasting covenant, to be God to you and to your offspring after you" (Gen. 17:7).

That covenant promise is not limited to the Jewish descendants of Abraham, but it is for Abraham's true descendants—all those God calls from every nation and in every time to be His covenant people: "For the promise is for you and for your children and for all who are far off, everyone whom the Lord our God calls to himself" (Acts 2:39). The promise is for believers and their children within the context of the covenant family. By God's grace, believers are adopted into the family of God and become part of His covenant: "You are the sons of the prophets and of the covenant that God made with your fathers" (Acts 3:25a). God's covenant promises are for believers *and* their children.

God promises never to "leave you or destroy you or forget the covenant . . ." (Deut. 4:31). His covenant faithfulness extends to all generations of believers: "Know therefore that the LORD your God is God, the faithful God who keeps covenant and steadfast love with those who love him and keep his commandments, to a thousand generations" (Deut. 7:9). God's love isn't for only one generation of believers, but is also for their succeeding children—even to a thousand generations!

The book of Psalms, so full of assurance to believers who have lost loved ones, promises believers God's "friendship" with them through His covenant: "The friendship of the LORD is for those who fear him, and he makes known to them his covenant" (Ps. 25:14). The prophet Isaiah assures us that God's covenant love is permanent: "'For the mountains may depart and the hills be removed, but my steadfast love shall not depart from you, and my covenant of peace shall not be removed,' says the LORD, who has compassion on you" (Isa. 54:10). Even when earthquakes level mountains, crumble cities, and crush people, God's love and His peace stand firm with His children.

God promises to be a faithful and loving God to believers, but believers are to listen to God's Word and obey the commands of His covenant: "Now, therefore, if you will indeed obey my voice and keep my covenant, you shall be my treasured possession among all peoples, for all the earth is mine" (Ex. 19:5). The God who owns the whole earth treasures obedient believers as His own precious possession. Psalm 103 beautifully conveys the promise and obligation of the covenant in a generational context: "But the steadfast love of the Lord is from everlasting to everlasting on those who fear him, and his righteousness to children's children, to those who keep his covenant and remember to do his commandments" (vv. 17–18).

These Old Testament passages emphasize God's faithful love to believers and their children throughout their generations. The New Testament continues God's covenantal promises and stresses their fulfillment through Christ's perfect obedience. Christ reaffirmed the covenant when He instituted the sacrament of Holy Communion. During the last supper with His disciples, Christ spoke of the wine as His "blood of the covenant" (Matt. 26:28, Mark 14:24). With Christ's self-sacrifice for our salvation, God's covenant relationship with His people entered into a new manifestation. "This is the covenant that I will make with them after those days, declares the Lord; I will put my laws on their hearts, and write them on their minds" (Heb. 10:16). The new covenant is more intimate than the old covenant. Through the Spirit of Christ dwelling in us, God puts His law on our hearts and writes it on our minds.

The shedding of human blood began when Cain killed Abel (Gen. 4:8). Christ gave Himself up so that through the shedding of His blood He would overcome Abel's shed blood and every subsequent sin. He is the mediator of a new covenant that surpasses the old covenant: ". . . Jesus, the mediator of a new covenant, and . . . the sprinkled blood that speaks a better word than the blood of Abel" (Heb. 12:24).

The covenant exists from Abel's death (recorded in Genesis) to Christ's return (depicted in Revelation). The covenant will come to its fullest expression when "God's temple in heaven" is opened and the ark of the *covenant* will appear (Rev. 11:19). God established His covenant in the Old Testament, Christ affirmed it in the New Testament, and God's covenant relationship with His people continues into the future, when it will be enjoyed in all its fullness after Christ's return. Using the marriage analogy, one could say that the marriage vows were spoken in the Old Testament, the marriage license was signed in the New Testament, and the marriage will be consummated at Christ's return.

Children of believers are considered part of the covenant, even if one of their parents does not believe: "For the unbelieving husband is made holy because of his wife, and the unbelieving wife is made holy because of her husband. Otherwise your children would be unclean, but as it is, they are holy" (1 Cor. 7:14). God honors His covenant and loves the children of believers, even those in unequal marriages.

"And as for the resurrection of the dead, have you not read what was said to you by God: 'I am the God of Abraham, and the God of

Isaac, and the God of Jacob'? He is not God of the dead, but of the living" (Matt. 22:31–32). We can have comfort from knowing that even our children who have died still live in His presence. Parents grieving the loss of a little child can draw immense comfort from their intimate relationship with God. Within this covenantal relationship, God promises to love believers *and* their children.

16: Confessional Comfort

The biblical emphasis on God's ovenant comforts parents grieving the loss of an infant. God's promises are sure, and His covenantal love is a secure anchor for those who grieve. Parents may also be comforted by Reformed confessions that help explain biblical and covenantal concepts. The Canons of Dort comprise a Reformed confession that beautifully articulate comfort to believers who lose an infant. It is one of three documents, known as the Three Forms of Unity, embraced by churches in the Reformed tradition. The other two documents are the Belgic Confession and the Heidelberg Catechism.

The comfort that comes from the Canons of Dort becomes even more meaningful when one understands a bit of the history and purpose of this document. In the seventeenth century, a controversy arose in the Dutch churches regarding teachings advocated by followers of Jacob Arminius. In opposition to the Reformed understanding of the Bible, these followers published a protest document or Remonstrance in 1610, which promoted five of their teachings: the free will of man due to only partial depravity, election based on foreseen faith, universal atonement, the ability to resist saving grace, and the possibility of a lapse from saving grace.[1]

The Synod of Dort, comprised of theologians from the Netherlands as well as eight other countries, met in 1618–19 to respond to the threat of Arminianism. The Synod crafted the Canons of Dort, which affirmed five Reformed teachings in response to the five Arminian teachings. These five doctrines are popularly known under the acronym of TULIP: Total depravity, Unconditional election,

---

1. The Remonstrance of 1610 declared that further study was required before they could conclude whether or not a lapse from saving grace was possible. When the Remonstrants defended their points at the Synod of Dort, they had concluded that a lapse was indeed possible.

Limited atonement, Irresistible grace, and Perseverance (or better, Preservation) of the saints.

The conclusion of the Canons shows that Arminians not only strayed from classic Reformed theology but also leveled several false accusations against traditional doctrines. One of the most disturbing charges was that the Reformed doctrine of election would mean that many "infant children of believers are snatched in their innocence from their mothers' breasts and cruelly cast into hell."[2] What an accusation! Imagine the emotional impact of this statement on grieving parents, particularly in seventeenth century society with its high rate of infant mortality. No wonder the Synod of Dort felt compelled to specifically address such a charge! Synod addressed it under the Canons' first main point of doctrine, "Divine Election and Reprobation," in Article 17, "The Salvation of the Infants of Believers":

> Since we must make judgments about God's will from His Word, which testifies that the children of believers are holy, not by nature but by virtue of the gracious covenant in which they together with their parents are included, godly parents ought not to doubt the election and salvation of their children whom God calls out of this life in infancy.[3]

When God takes an infant from this life, believing parents "ought not to doubt" the salvation of the child God has called home. The writers of Article 17 were careful to show that this judgment was based on the covenantal promises of God's Word.

An earlier translation of the Canons of Dort includes under Article 17 parenthetical references to Genesis 17:7, Acts 2:39, and 1 Corinthians 7:14.[4] Genesis 17:7 is God's covenantal promise to Abraham and all his descendants; Acts 2:39 is Peter's affirmation, in his Pentecost sermon, of God's covenantal promise for believers and their children; and 1 Corinthians 7:14 is the source for Article 17's language regarding the holiness of children by virtue of the covenant. Each of these texts was examined in the previous chapter within the

---

2. The quotation is on page 948 in the 1987 *Psalter Hymnal* by CRC Publications; Grand Rapids, MI. The entire Canons of Dort are found on pages 927–949.

3. Article 17 is on page 930 of the 1987 *Psalter Hymnal*.

4. Article 17 of the earlier translation appears on page 95 in the "Doctrinal Standards" section at the back of the 1976 *Psalter Hymnal*.

context of covenantal comfort. God's covenantal promises are for believers and their children. Believers who lose an infant can draw comfort from the biblical promises regarding the covenant. The writers of the Canons affirmed that covenantal belief must be based on God's Word, and that believing parents can trust God's gracious covenantal promises. Rather than falling into the fearful imagery painted by Arminian accusations, the Canons' affirmation of God's Word conveys the pastoral imagery of the littlest lamb being lifted into the loving arms of the Good Shepherd (Isa. 40:11).

Dr. Cornelis P. Venema writes, "The remarkable feature of Article I/17 is that it expresses a full confidence regarding God's favor toward such children. Sovereign and merciful election, far from casting a shadow over the question of assurance, undergirds and fuels a robust confidence in God's favor toward the children of believers."[5] Dr. Venema concludes: "In the specific case of the deceased children of believing parents, the authors of the Canons desired a clear statement of assurance that would comfort parents and belie the false accusation of the Arminian party . . . The affirmation of Article I/17 declares that God's sovereign and merciful election is the only basis for assurance regarding the salvation of the deceased infant children of believers . . . As members of the fallen race in Adam, the children of believers whom God calls out of this life in infancy are saved solely by virtue of God's gracious favor. Far from intimating any doubt respecting the assurance of their election, this article declares an assurance securely founded upon the biblical and Reformed teaching regarding election . . . [This] teaching safeguards the singular honor of God who sovereignly and graciously saves His people in Christ, and it undergirds the believer's confidence in His gracious and invincible favor."[6] The Canons of Dort assure grieving parents and assuage nagging doubts.

---

5. Dr. Venema's quotation is from page 1 of "Election of Infants: A Study of Canons of Dort Article I/17," *Reformed Pathways,* insert to Mid-America Reformed Seminary's newsletter, the *Messenger,* Vol. 26, No. 3.

6. Dr. Venema's second quotation is found on page 4 of the *Reformed Pathways* insert in the Vol. 26, No. 3 *Messenger.* Although I agree with Dr. Venema's vigorous interpretation of Article I/17, some theologians in the past as well as in the present interpret this article of the Canons differently, believing that the Bible does not speak specifically enough to the matter to draw this confident conclusion.

The oldest of the Three Forms of Unity, the Belgic Confession, arose out of intense persecution under the Roman Catholic government of the Netherlands in the sixteenth century. Guido de Brès, the primary author of the Belgic Confession and a pastor of the Reformed churches in the Netherlands, died a martyr's death in 1567, only six years after he wrote the Confession in 1561. The Confession was written to demonstrate that Reformed believers were peaceable citizens and biblical Christians. Although it did not stem the tide of immediate persecution, it became a significant and comprehensive statement of the Reformed faith that still speaks to believers today.

Its affirmation regarding the infant children of believers appears within the context of Article 34's discussion of baptism: "We believe our children ought to be baptized and sealed with the sign of the covenant, as little children were circumcised in Israel on the basis of the same promises made to our children. And truly, Christ has shed his blood no less for washing the little children of believers than he did for adults."[7] The Belgic Confession asserts that infants should be baptized as a sign of the covenant, just as infants had been circumcised under the old administration of the covenant. It emphasizes that Christ's atonement is as fully effective for the salvation of the infant children of believers as it is for adults.

The Heidelberg Catechism, the third of the Three Forms of Unity, was first published in 1563 and continues to be used widely for instruction in the Reformed faith. It affirms the salvation of infants by echoing the language of the Belgic Confession in its Q. and A. 74 on baptism: "Infants as well as adults are in God's covenant and are his people. They, no less than adults, are promised the forgiveness of sin through Christ's blood and the Holy Spirit who produces faith."[8] Believing parents can cling with confidence to God's biblical and covenantal promises expressed in these Reformed confessions. They can rest in the assurance that our covenant God takes even

---

7. The quotation from Article 34 of the Belgic Confession is on page 852 of the 1987 *Psalter Hymnal*. The text of the entire Belgic Confession appears from pages 817–859. An earlier translation can be found on pages 69–90 in the "Doctrinal Standards" section at the back of the 1976 *Psalter Hymnal*.

8. The answer to Q. 74 of the Heidelberg Catechism can be found on page 892 of the 1987 *Psalter Hymnal* and on page 35 at the back of the 1976 *Psalter Hymnal*.

the littlest lambs in His loving arms and tenderly carries them to greener pastures.

17: Only Comfort

Believers who take God at His Word can find comfort in God's biblical and covenantal promises as well as in the explanations of those promises found in the Reformed confessions. One facet of those confessions deserves a closer look. The first question and answer of the Heidelberg Catechism is a well known and much loved confession that beautifully conveys the comfort of Christ's sufficiency:

1 Q. What is your only comfort in life and in death?
A. That I am not my own,
but belong—
body and soul,
in life and in death—
to my faithful Savior Jesus Christ.
He has fully paid for all my sins with his precious blood,
and has set me free from the tyranny of the devil.
He also watches over me in such a way
that not a hair can fall from my head
without the will of my Father in heaven:
in fact, all things must work together for my salvation.
Because I belong to him,
Christ, by his Holy Spirit,
assures me of eternal life
and makes me whole-heartedly willing and ready
from now on to live for him.[1]

That first question and answer of the Heidelberg Catechism reflect the theme of comfort that is woven throughout the Catechism. Many people memorize Q. and A. 1 and treasure it in their hearts. Little children can recite the first part of it. Young people professing their

---

1. This question and answer are found on page 8 at the back of the 1976 *Psalter Hymnal* by CRC Publications; Grand Rapids, MI, where the solid biblical basis is established by no fewer than ten Scripture references.

faith before the elders of their church claim it as their favorite question and answer. Elderly folks who have forgotten nearly everything—even the names of their own children—still remember it. It is often printed in the folders handed out at funerals.

Why is this question and answer so meaningful to so many? It is meaningful because it poignantly expresses God's love. And it is meaningful because it faithfully conveys biblical truth. We read in 1 Corinthians 6:19–20, "You are not your own, for you were bought with a price." That price was the precious blood of Christ, shed for your sins and mine. If you believe Jesus died to pay for your sin, you don't belong to yourself. You belong to Jesus Christ your Savior who faithfully served God in His life and by His death.

The catechism answer reflects this truth by saying, "I am not my own, but belong—body and soul, in life and in death—to my faithful Savior Jesus Christ." Through the ages, the idea of "belonging" has been abused by those with power or authority to force others to serve them, but that is not what it means to belong to Christ. Belonging to Christ is the exact opposite of slavery or abuse. Belonging to Christ is the only way to live a joyful and fulfilled life in true freedom from oppression or exploitation. Only the believer who belongs to Christ is free from the guilt of sin and the penalty of hell. Only the believer who belongs to Christ is lovingly cared for as a precious son or daughter. Only the believer is safe and secure for all eternity.

Jesus says in John 10:28, "I give them eternal life, and they will never perish, and no one will snatch them out of my hand." Nothing and no one in this wicked world can pry us from the strong hand of Christ. He will never let us slip from his grip. We may have sorrow and pain, but Christ is always holding us securely, like a loving father holding a child's hand as they walk across a slippery bridge.

Romans 14:8 says, "For if we live, we live to the Lord, and if we die, we die to the Lord. So then, whether we live or whether we die, we are the Lord's." Whether believers live or die, they are the Lord's. In that knowledge, we are able to live with joy and die without fear. Through all the struggles in this sad world and even when we face death—whether it is our own or that of a child—we have the comfort of knowing that we and our covenant children belong—body and soul—to Christ.

The answer to Heidelberg Catechism Q. 1 continues with a beautiful explanation of why we belong to Christ and what's so good about that:

> He has fully paid for all my sins with his precious blood,
> and has set me free from the tyranny of the devil.
> He also watches over me in such a way
> that not a hair can fall from my head
> without the will of my Father in heaven:
> in fact, all things must work together for my salvation.

Because Christ has paid for our sins with His blood, we are no longer slaves to sin and its tyrant, the devil. We have been set free! Our freedom isn't an aimless wandering, like lost children with no one to care for them. Christ is actively watching over us and working out all the events of our lives, even to the smallest detail—like the number of hairs left in your brush each morning.

This language is not based on mere positive thinking; it is the language of Scripture. Matthew 10:30 says, "But even the hairs of your head are all numbered." And Luke 21:18 says, "But not a hair of your head will perish." That assurance from Luke is within the context of a warning about persecution. If God preserves every hair on the head of each persecuted believer, He will certainly preserve and protect His children and their covenant children throughout their entire lives, no matter how long or how short those lives may be. If not one hair can fall to your shoulder apart from God's will, you can be sure that a child's life cannot fail apart from God's will. Even the loss of a child is somehow part of the way "all things must work together" for good for those who believe. This language reflects Romans 8:28, which was discussed at the beginning of chapter 14. This beautiful answer of the Heidelberg Catechism concludes with the logical acknowledgement that those who belong to Christ will receive assurance from the Holy Spirit that their future—and that of their covenant children—is eternally secure.

What should be our response to God's beautiful promises of faithful love and care in this life and eternal security in the next? The only appropriate response to such marvelous assurance is for us to be "whole-heartedly willing and ready" to live for Him! Christ has given His covenant children eternal life. In this world, filled with sickness and sorrow, you and your covenant children are safe in the arms of Jesus. When God takes His children from this world to their eternal home in heaven, whether after a long life with laughter and weeping, or after a short life without even drawing a breath, believers and their covenant children are safe in the arms of Jesus. We are always safe in the arms of Jesus. What wonderful comfort we have in Christ's promise that we are not our own, but belong to Him!

Part Five: Grieving with Hope

18: Hopeful Grief

Since the Bible affirms the personhood of the unborn child, a loss at any point before or after birth (or the loss of never conceiving) can be devastating and may be grieved. Those who have stifled their grief—for whatever reason—can be assured that grief is a natural reaction to loss. They can be free to grieve. The Christian faith is the solid rock that keeps believers from suffocating in life's miry pits of despair. But faith doesn't insulate from tragedy or prevent its ensuing grief. Believers grieve. Grief is not inherently sinful. When Job's children died in a progressive series of great losses, Job grieved. He expressed his grief by tearing his robe, shaving his head, and falling on the ground. The Bible specifically relates that "in all this Job did not sin" (Job 1:22). When Jesus' friend Lazarus died, He wept (John 11:35). These are two prime biblical examples demonstrating that grief is not a sinful reaction to loss.

But believers do not grieve without hope. Paul writes, "Brothers, we do not want you to be ignorant about those who fall asleep, or to grieve like the rest of men, who have no hope" (1 Thess. 4:13, NIV84). Paul isn't suggesting that Christians ignore or stifle grief. He assumes that they will grieve the loss of a loved one, but he wants them to grieve as believers. He wants them to grieve with hope.

That hope is not based on the fickle feelings, the puny strength, or the finite minds of human beings. That hope is firmly grounded in the unfailing affection, the almighty power, and the sovereign knowledge of God. The Word of this loving, omnipotent, and omniscient God is sure. That sure Word is Christ. Through Him, God broke the power of sin and the grip of death. God became man, the perfection of divinity and humanity, in Jesus Christ. He lived in perfect obedience to God, He took the guilt of sinners upon Himself, He paid for that sin through His atoning death on the cross, He vanquished death by rising from the grave, and He ascended to heaven where He sovereignly reigns at God's right hand. This Christ is the same yesterday and today and forever (Heb. 13:8).

Because Christ has been raised, believers look with hope to the resurrection of themselves and their loved ones—no matter at what stage of life God takes them home. In his first letter to the troublesome church in Corinth, Paul writes at length about the futility of faith if Christ has not been raised (15:12–19). But he doesn't end there. He adds, "But in fact Christ has been raised from the dead, the firstfruits of those who have fallen asleep." The "firstfruits" in the Old Testament represented the first and best of the harvest that was consecrated to God. Christ is the first and best of the resurrected bodies of all believers. Paul continues, "Christ the firstfruits, then at his coming those who belong to Christ" (1 Cor. 15:20, 23). The believer's hope for the resurrection is sure. Christ's resurrection is an infallible guarantee of humanity's future resurrection.

As he continues, Paul uses an agricultural analogy that brings to mind the undeveloped unborn. He writes of sowing the "bare kernel" that "is not the body that is to be," but "God gives it a body as he has chosen" (1 Cor. 15:37–38). The tiniest unborn child may not even be formed into a recognizable shape, but God recognizes this child. He chose to give this child life, and He chose to take this child home, even if its tiny body is still undeveloped or at an early stage of life.

Paul continues with contrasts that seem particularly appropriate to the loss of infant children: "What is sown is perishable; what is raised is imperishable . . . It is sown in weakness; it is raised in power. It is sown a natural body; it is raised a spiritual body" (1 Cor. 15:42–44). What could be more perishable, weak, and natural than an infant? Yet, one day, this tiny infant's body will be raised as imperishable, powerful, and spiritual.

Because of that hope in the resurrection, Paul urges fellow believers to "be steadfast, immovable, always abounding in the work of the Lord, knowing that in the Lord your labor is not in vain" (1 Cor. 15:58). Undoubtedly "labor" here refers to the believer's work in God's kingdom. But couldn't the contractions of childbirth be considered as part of a mother's "labor" for the Lord? Certainly the text cannot be limited to this meaning, but I believe it is legitimate for a mother to view her "labor" in childbirth as part of her life's work for the Lord. Even if that labor does not bring extended time with an anticipated baby, God assures believers that "labor" for Him "is not in vain." In some inexplicable way, even this was part of God's sovereign plan for the lives of the mother *and* the child.

Believers realize that children are wonderful gifts with an eternal future, but we care for our children only as temporary stewards. Job accepted the death of his children as God's will for his life. By God's grace, he was equipped with the hope that enabled him to worship God in spite of his grief. He said, "Naked I came from my mother's womb, and naked shall I return. The LORD gave, and the LORD has taken away; blessed be the name of the LORD" (Job 1:21).

Job had a full-orbed understanding of the beginning and the end of life. He realized that he had begun his life on earth as a naked and helpless baby without any possessions. He also realized that he would end his life on earth as a naked and helpless body without anything he could claim as his own. Job realized that every camel and ox and donkey was a temporary gift from God. Even his dearly loved children, for whom he continually offered sacrifices and sought forgiveness (Job 1:5), were only temporarily under his care. He knew he was a steward.

Later in this quintessential account of suffering, Job proclaims a marvelous testimony to his faith in a living Christ. His profession encompasses his belief in Christ's second coming and his belief in the bodily resurrection of the dead.

> For I know that my Redeemer lives,
>
> And He shall stand at last on the earth;
>
> And after my skin is destroyed, this I know,
>
> That in my flesh I shall see God,
>
> Whom I shall see for myself,
>
> And my eyes shall behold, and not another.
>
> How my heart yearns within me! (Job 19:25–27, NKJV)

Before Christ's first advent as a helpless baby in a manger, Job confessed that his Redeemer lived and would stand on this earth.

Job confessed that his own skin would be destroyed, but on the great day of Christ's return it would be resurrected with power. In his own flesh, Job would see God. The pupils of his eyes would contract as he would focus on the brightness of Christ. No wonder his heart yearned within him!

Just as Job longed for the day when his resurrected body and glorified eyes would see his Redeemer, believers can long with certain hope that our bodies—and the bodies of believing loved ones—will be gloriously resurrected. Our hope in the loss of a loved one, even one whom we did not have much opportunity to love, is that one day the glorious and perfected bodies of all of God's children will be raised to enjoy perfect fellowship with each other and with Christ. Christ's resurrection was the "firstfruits"—the first and best resurrection—that guarantees the future resurrection of our glorified bodies.

19: Guilty Grief

A baby is a baby. That's why a loss before birth, although it may not be as devastating as a loss during or after birth, is still a loss and may be grieved. This doesn't mean, however, that a loss at any stage must be grieved. Some mothers may well be able to accept a miscarriage and go on with life without either resorting to denial or succumbing to grief. Some miscarriages are far less traumatic than others. Parents shouldn't necessarily feel guilty for a lack of grief. Every situation is different, and every person handles loss differently.

On the other hand, some mothers may be overwhelmed with grief that is compounded by guilt. Perhaps they had difficulty accepting an unexpected pregnancy that was subsequently lost. Perhaps they blame themselves by thinking that some activity during pregnancy led to the death of their child. Perhaps they are tormented by past sins and can't help thinking that the child's death was their just punishment.

Ironically, reading certain Scripture passages may actually compound this guilt. A mother feeling guilty over her initial difficulty in accepting a pregnancy may feel increased guilt when reading passages that speak of children as a heritage from the Lord. A mother feeling that she failed in her trust to carry a pregnancy full term may feel additional guilt when reading passages emphasizing childbearing as a means to advance God's kingdom. And a mother regretting past sin may be further burdened with guilt when reading passages that appear to contrast the blessing of life for obedience with the curse of death for disobedience. A closer look is in order.

Scripture clearly teaches that children are a blessing from the Lord. The Psalms, which are a precious source of comfort in a time of loss, also speak powerfully about the blessing of children. Psalm 113 speaks of how God "gives the barren woman a home, making her the joyous mother of children" (v. 9). Psalm 127:3–5 depicts the blessing of children: "Children are a heritage from the LORD," and "the fruit of the womb a reward." Children are compared to "arrows in the hand of a warrior;" the man is "blessed" whose "quiver" is full. These archery images are quickly followed by the agricultural images of Psalm 128, where a wife is compared to "a fruitful vine" and children to "olive shoots" around the family table (vv. 3–6). Grieving parents may feel weighed down by guilt when reading such passages. They need to be reminded that—even if they initially failed to appreciate the anticipated child—God decreed the number of this child's days before conception.

In Psalm 139, which speaks so beautifully of God knitting together the unborn child, David writes: "All the days ordained for me were written in your book before one of them came to be" (v. 16, NIV84). Before the mother's reaction to her pregnancy, before she even began to suspect she was pregnant, God had already determined when that child would be called home. God sovereignly ordains the life and the death of each person. Psalm 37:18 tells us that the "LORD knows the days of the blameless." Before any child was conceived, God knew the exact number of that child's days. No matter when God takes a child from this life, whether early or late in a pregnancy, before or after birth, the number of that child's days has been ordained by God.

The perception about the responsibility to bear children in obedience to God and to further His kingdom has validity since this is a foundational concept from the beginning of Scripture. God's command to Adam and Eve was to "be fruitful and multiply" (Gen. 1:28). Old Testament mothers longed for children as a sign of God's blessing and to bring the chosen line closer to the coming Messiah. Bearing children was important to the patriarchs' wives—so important that Rachel demanded Jacob "give her children" or she would die. He rightly asked, "Am I in the place of God who has kept you from having children?" (Gen. 30:1–2, NIV84). Jacob acknowledged God's sovereignty in bestowing or withholding the blessing of birth.

The longing for the Messiah was fulfilled in Christ, who embraced children and said, "Let the little children come to me, and do not hinder them, for the kingdom of heaven belongs to such as these"

(Matt. 19:14, Mark 10:14, Luke 18:16, NIV84). Even though Christ has come as the promised Messiah who blesses little children, the concept of having children as a covenantal responsibility remains. Christian parents still believe that the birth of every covenant child adds to God's kingdom. Parents who feel as if they've somehow failed in their covenantal responsibilities must realize that their child—no matter when he or she was taken from them—is still part of God's kingdom. They need to remember God's sovereignty in this bitter providence.

A deeply embedded Old Testament paradigm is that of blessings for obedience and curses for disobedience. Before Moses hands the reins of leadership to Joshua, he admonishes the people at length, including the injunction: "Now choose life, so that you and your children may live" (Deut. 30:19, NIV84). Many other passages in Deuteronomy promise long life and blessing for believers and their children who obey God's commands (6:2, 11:21, 7:12–14, 12:28). In the Ten Commandments and other readings of the law, however, children are to be punished for the sins of the fathers to the third and fourth generation (Exodus 20:5; 34:7; Num. 14:18; Deut. 5:9).

Blessing and curse were directly linked with childbearing in the stories of Hannah and Michal. Hannah was blessed with children for her faithfulness (1 Sam. 1), while Michal was cursed with barrenness for her unfaithfulness (2 Sam. 6:23). Adultery is linked to barrenness in Numbers 5:28, which states that only the woman free from adultery will be able to bear children. David's double sins of adultery and murder were punished by the death of the child Bathsheba bore (2 Sam. 12). Cursory readings of such passages could make a parent feel as if the loss of a child is punishment for personal sin. Except for Christ, everyone who has ever lived on earth is a sinner (Ps. 14:1–3; 53:1–13; Rom. 3:10–12). And we live in a sinful world. Every person is a sinner, but not every tragedy is punishment for sin.

Job is the ultimate example of a righteous man whose suffering was not a punishment. Although his "comforters" were right about the inherent sinfulness of man and the sovereign righteousness of God, they erred when they accused Job of secret sin. Job was not being punished for his sin. His suffering stands through the ages as a powerful testimony of God's sovereignty and love in the midst of tragedy.

The biblical emphasis on the blessing of children, the covenantal responsibility to bear children, and the doctrine of punishment for sin may sharpen the grief believing parents feel after the loss of an infant. But it's important to remember that the loss of a child is a result of sin, not a punishment for sin. Our world is weighed down with the effects of sin, but tragedies are not usually direct punishment for personal sin.

It's also important to remember that there is forgiveness for every sordid sin that lurks in the shadowy past. After confession and repentance, the Christian must cling to God's promised forgiveness. Psalm 103:12 assures us that "as far as the east is from the west, so far does he remove our transgressions from us." God removes our sin far from us for the sake of Christ. He paid the penalty for all our sins and substituted His perfect life for each of our sin-ridden lives. Believers should live with an awareness of sin and daily repent from specific sins, but believing parents shouldn't allow a false sense of guilt to compound what may be an already overwhelming sense of grief after the loss of an infant.

20: Being Forgiven

The general discussion of guilt in the last chapter noted that suffering is not usually a result of an individual's personal sin, but it *is always* the result of the world's pervasive sin. Believers can be assured that God forgives the repentant sinner. Parents who recognize and repent from sin shouldn't compound their grief with needless guilt.

Adultery was briefly mentioned and other sexual sins were implied in that discussion, which are certainly sins that can be forgiven by God's grace. But a bit more needs to be said about being forgiven, because some past sins can have a powerful effect on the grief associated with the loss of an infant. Few sins are free from consequences, but there are generally far-reaching and heartrending consequences for sexual sin. A husband or wife who has been sexually active before or outside the covenant of marriage, as well as a woman who has had an abortion, may face extraordinary challenges in coping with the loss of a child. This parent may find it difficult not to link the loss with earlier experiences. Those experiences may have caused a host of unresolved issues of which the parent may not even be aware. Promiscuity and abortion can contribute to chronic emotional struggles such as anxiety and depression that greatly complicate the grieving process.

This suffering parent needs extra assurance about the forgiveness of sins. The parent who has strayed sexually needs the reassurance of forgiveness and restoration. And the woman who has chosen abortion needs to know that God forgives even this sin. Anyone who repents of past sins can cling to the many biblical promises of forgiveness. Christ Himself assures the repentant sinner of the comprehensive scope of forgiveness. He says, "Truly I say to you, all sins will be forgiven . . ." (Mark 3:28). Matthew also records this assurance of Christ: "Therefore I tell you, every sin and blasphemy will be forgiven people, but the blasphemy against the Spirit will not be forgiven" (Matt. 12:31).

All kinds of sexual sin and even the sin of abortion are forgiven through God's grace and the atoning work of Christ. The only sin that will not be forgiven is blasphemy against the Spirit (see also Mark 3:29 and Luke 12:10). This sin has become popularly known as the unforgivable or unpardonable sin, but what is it really? It might be helpful to start with what the unforgivable sin is not. It is not promiscuity. It is not adultery. It is not homosexuality. It is not abortion. It is not suicide. It is not murder. All of these are sins that can be forgiven. It is not even denial of Christ. John 21:15–19 demonstrates that Christ forgave Peter of this grievous sin.

The context of the Matthew and Mark passages speaking about the unforgivable sin makes it clear that this sin involves the kind of hardness and impenitence that blasphemes in the face of clear demonstrations of the triune God's divinity. Matthew Henry writes, "This blasphemy is excepted, not for any defect of mercy in God, or merit in Christ, but because it inevitably leaves the sinner in infidelity and unrepentance."[1] In other words, this sin alone is the exception to forgiveness, not because God's grace or Christ's merit are insufficient, but because this sin indicates the complete impenitence of the heart. In the same paragraph, Henry goes on to say, "Those who fear they have committed this sin, give a good sign that they have not."[2]

Henry is echoing what earlier theologians taught regarding the unforgivable sin. Augustine defined "blasphemy against the Spirit" as "impenitence" in the face of God's grace. He said, "Against this gratuitous gift, against this grace of God, does the impenitent heart speak."[3] John Calvin agreed that the unforgivable sin involves a direct rejection of the Spirit. He wrote that the person who purposefully "endeavors to extinguish the offered light of the Spirit" will not be pardoned.[4] Although commentators and theologians may differ slightly in their definitions of the unforgivable sin, it is clear that this sin involves a blatant rejection of the Spirit by the unrepentant heart, a sin impossible for a repentant Christian to commit.

---

1. Matthew Henry's *Commentary,* Chap. 12, vv. 22–37, V.1.2.

2. *Commentary,* Chap. 12, vv. 22–37, V.1.2.

3. *A Select Library of the Nicene and Post-Nicene Fathers of the Christian Church,* Vol. 6. p. 325.

4. *Institutes of the Christian Religion,* Ch. 5, Sec. 7.

The believing parent who struggles with assurance of forgiveness for past sins needs to be reminded of the comprehensive scope of God's forgiveness. All sexual sin and the sin of abortion can be forgiven through Christ's complete atoning sacrifice. Due to the special nature of some sins, however, a parent who struggles with the past may need professional counseling to help identify and overcome emotional problems or guilty feelings that complicate grief. If professional assistance is pursued, it ought to be sought from a Christian counselor who understands God's forgiveness and sovereignty as well as human emotions and psychology. Secular counseling will fail to bring the comfort of God's forgiveness into the equation.

But some forms of Christian counseling may fail to bring the benefit of psychology's expertise into the equation. Some Christian counseling methods are too simplistic, blaming personal sin for every emotional problem and urging the sufferer to search for a specific sin at the root of each problem. Such methods sometimes neglect to present fully the comfort of forgiveness. They may fail to assist the sufferer with legitimate coping techniques from the field of psychology or necessary medications from a physician. Christian counseling that is too simplistic often ends up beating the sufferer over the head with the plank of sin instead of laying it down as a bridge over the emotional chasm. The parent suffering grief that is complicated by guilt over sin lurking in the past may need to seek Christian counseling that employs a balanced perspective to equip this parent with the necessary spiritual, emotional, or medical tools.

Whether or not counseling is necessary, the parent whose grief is complicated by guilt must cling to God's promises of forgiveness. One of those promises is found in Colossians 2:13: "And you, who were dead in your trespasses and the uncircumcision of your flesh, God made alive together with him, having forgiven us all our trespasses." Although we were "dead" in our past sins, God made us "alive" with Him. He has forgiven not "some" or "part" or "a few that were not so bad," but "all" our sins.

This comprehensive assurance echoes an Old Testament promise recorded by Jeremiah: "I will cleanse them from *all* the guilt of their sin against me, and I will forgive *all* the guilt of their sin and rebellion against me" (33:8, emphasis added). Jeremiah also communicates the finality of God's forgiveness: "For I will forgive their iniquity, and I remember their sin no more" (31:34). For the sake of His Son's atoning sacrifice, God no longer bears our sins in His mind. If God is willing to put our sins out of His mind, shouldn't we forbid false guilt a foothold in our minds?

A wonderful demonstration of forgiveness for sin is found in Luke's story of the woman who anointed Jesus' feet. The host, a Pharisee, thinks, "If this man were a prophet, he would have known who and what sort of woman this is who is touching him, for she is a sinner" (Luke 7:39). Jesus knows the Pharisee's thoughts and tells him a parable to demonstrate His point about forgiveness. He concludes, "Therefore I tell you, her sins, which are many, are forgiven—for she loved much. But he who is forgiven little, loves little" (v. 47). Then, turning to the woman, Jesus directly assures her, "Your sins are forgiven" (v. 48). And that is His final word to all repentant sinners.

21: Forgiving Others

Since God forgives the repentant sinner, parents who recognize and repent from sin shouldn't allow guilt—even the tenacious guilt of past sin—to complicate their grief. God completely forgives all past sins of those who repent. In cases of abuse or accident, however, grief can be additionally complicated. In both of these cases, the grieving person struggles with pain caused by someone else's behavior. Abuse can be sexual, physical, emotional, or verbal (frequently a combination of two or more). It is an intentional, and often repeated, abuse of power or authority. It is not limited temporarily to the pain it inflicts on a child; it permanently scars a person for life. Even as adults, victims of abuse continue to struggle with overwhelming fear, devastating anxiety, and crushing depression. The pain from the past that haunts them is not their choice or their fault. They suffer not because of their own sin, but because of someone else's sin against them. They have been victims. They continue to face the possibility of victimization since predators sense their vulnerability and attempt to prey on them. Persons who have suffered from abuse will almost certainly face a complex burden of grief following the loss of an infant.

Similar to the parents discussed in the previous chapter, parents with abuse in their past may link the loss of their tiny child to earlier experiences. They, too, may not realize the extent of issues complicating their grief. They may feel an unwarranted measure of guilt or responsibility for both their past and present pain. They may feel anger without even knowing if it's directed at themselves, the past perpetrator, present family members, or at God. They may be fearful or depressed. Chronic anxiety or depression may require counseling from a compassionate pastor or a godly therapist.

Professional counselor Joyce De Haan notes that the loss of an infant is "greatly complicated" when the mother has experienced sexual abuse. She reminds abused women of God's sovereignty, often using the previously discussed Romans 8:28. "All brokenness, consequences of repentant sin and other sin committed against us will be used for the good of those who are in the Lord Jesus Christ," she says. "Suffering in the Christian life draws us closer to our Heavenly Father."

"I think that the story of the man blind from birth is especially helpful," she adds, referring to the healing described in John 9. "This story demonstrates that brokenness and sadness happen for God's glory and power to be revealed." God can and does manifest His glory and His power in the midst of life's most painful brokenness. Loss can bring the grieving person closer to God. It can make a person more compassionate toward others. Even if we don't see a reason or result, we can trust God and take Him at His Word. He is sovereign over all the events of our lives; He will somehow use our pain for our good and His glory.

In contrast to abuse, an accident is an unintentional, one-time action, and is not an abuse of power or authority. Although not common, it happens that a pregnant woman is involved in an accident—perhaps someone runs a red light or pulls out in front of her vehicle—and she loses her baby. The pain of grief is complicated by anger toward the person who caused the accident. The one who experiences loss feels like a victim. When accidental death occurs, the levels of culpability and the degrees of remorse vary. Perhaps the driver looked both ways before pulling out, but her vision was obscured; now she has nightmares and is overwhelmed with sorrow. Perhaps the driver had been drinking and his judgment was clouded; now he expresses no remorse and continues to drink and drive. In either case, or in any of the many possible scenarios between, the accident was not a premeditated action.

The parent who has experienced loss as the result of an accident also needs to recognize God's sovereignty and accept the biblical truth that all things work for good. But the person who experiences such a loss will almost certainly struggle with anger. Because God is sovereign over all that happens, anger toward others or railing at "fate" is really anger against God. In the final analysis, the person who caused the accident was only an instrument God used to take that child home. Recognizing God's sovereignty over even the devastating events of our lives is crucial for coping with the complex grief associated with abuse or accident. Prayer for God's grace is also crucial and will be discussed more in a later chapter. But the key that opens the door of healing for those who feel victimized is forgiving.

Christ taught believers to pray, "Forgive us our debts, as we also have forgiven our debtors" (Matt. 6:12). The debts mentioned here refer to more than mere money. Christ used a parable about an ungrateful servant to effectively demonstrate His teaching about forgiving others. The servant's master forgave him of a huge debt that would be impossible for anyone to pay. But the ungrateful servant went out and found a fellow servant who owed him only a small amount. He grabbed him and began to choke him, demanding, "Pay back what you owe me!" (Matt. 18:28). God has forgiven the impossible debt of our sin. He calls us to forgive those who have hurt us, whether the pain was unintended and trivial or deliberate and traumatic.

Our forgiving others doesn't necessarily mean that God has forgiven them. God does not forgive every sin—only those of repentant sinners who believe in Christ. Every sin must and will be paid for—either by Christ on the cross for the believer or by eternal torment in hell for the unbeliever. Our forgiveness doesn't absolve the perpetrator from guilt or responsibility. Those who have sinned against others should repent and seek reconciliation (although face-to-face reconciliation may not always be necessary or advisable). But even if there is no regret expressed or reconciliation attempted, forgiving someone who has hurt us is instrumental in healing.

A determination *not* to forgive doesn't hurt the person who caused pain. It does, however, provide the fertile soil in which the seed of bitterness takes root. That small seedling can quickly grow into a strapping sapling, which eventually becomes a sturdy sequoia. It is far better to keep the seed of bitterness from taking root. Forgiveness is a decision. But it isn't a decision that is made only once. Forgiving someone who has sinned against us is a continuing process. We need to remind ourselves repeatedly of our decision to forgive, initially perhaps several times a day—or several times each hour! We may need to remind ourselves periodically about our decision to forgive for the rest of our lives.

A decision to forgive is possible only by God's grace. Only God can give us the grace we need to forgive those who have hurt us. Forgiveness is never easy, but it is necessary. And God's grace is sufficient. As Christ hung dying on the cross, He asked His Father to forgive those who nailed Him there. If He forgave his murderers, shouldn't we forgive those who hurt us? The parent who has been a victim of abuse or accident will progress toward healing by accepting God's sovereignty and making a decision to forgive. That decision is possible only by God's abundant and sustaining grace.

22: Family Grief

Mothers are the most obvious sufferers when a baby dies. Medical personnel, family, and friends sometimes ignore fathers in interactions following loss. But the loss of an infant can be just as devastating to them. Siblings and grandparents also grieve. A father may attempt to cope with grief by immersing himself in work. He may feel that he has failed in his responsibility to provide and protect. He may feel helpless about his inability to help his wife cope with her grief.

"Watching my wife be broken over a loss and not being able to remedy the situation was very difficult," Brad says. "Men desire to protect, help, and nurture their wives. On top of that I had to deal with my own grieving." Although many people comforted Stephanie, fewer sought to comfort Brad. "The father is often alienated in these situations, since the greater concern is for the mother," he says. "Men in the church often fail in reaching out to other men who face any type of grief or suffering. I believe this is especially the case when we have not experienced much suffering in our own lives." Because of this lack of communication, Brad became absorbed with reading books dealing with infant loss or with God's absolute sovereignty. "This for me was an opportunity to let God be God," Brad says, "as He is the true Sovereign."

Part of the problem Brad encountered with a lack of communication was the perception that his family's stillborn loss was not significant. "A loss through miscarriage or stillbirth seems unimportant to many," he says. Brad encourages others to acknowledge the reality of the loss as well as the grief of the fathers. "It's real, and they stand in need of grace," he says. "Don't ignore the mention of their loss, even if only in an e-mail. Let them know their loss is very real and that you grieve with them. Pray with them and for them." He also encourages continued contact with grieving fathers: "Check in with them periodically. Offer your assistance, even well after a loss."

Just as fathers sometimes tend to be ignored during times of early infant loss, the grief experienced by siblings is often marginalized. Meri never knew her sister who would have been two years older, because Patricia died at only three months. Her younger sister Rebekah lived for only one hour. Her older brother Ben and Meri (sixteen and eleven at the time) were at the hospital when Rebekah was born and were able to see and hold her. "I remember it being very sad," Meri says. "I think it's very difficult for a child to see their parents sad. Normally parents are strong and can fix anything. My parents were crying all the time. They let me know, however, that it was okay to cry and be sad. It's important for parents to explain that to children because they don't necessarily know what feelings are 'right' or 'wrong.'"

Meri was grieving, too, but children sometimes react to grief by focusing on things that may seem trivial or strange to adults. Meri recalls feeling a need to know the color of Rebekah's eyes. She also remembers feeling compelled to stand on Rebekah's grave after she was buried. And she remembers wanting to return to school because that was "normal" and was in her "comfort zone."

"It's important for children to get back into a normal routine after losing a sibling," she says. "Even though it is very sad and very difficult for several months, kids need the normalcy in a reasonable amount of time." Although she was eleven years old, Meri says, "I didn't fully realize at the time what had happened. I knew that I had lost a sister, but at that point I didn't realize the effect it would have on me throughout my whole life." During childhood, Meri avoided talking about her sisters because she didn't want to make her parents sad. She also hated to hear friends complain about their sisters. "I remember thinking, 'Don't you know what you have? Be thankful you have a sister to fight with!'" she says. "It is something that I still struggle with from time to time."

"Before I was married," she adds, "another thing that was difficult was not knowing who the maid of honor would be in my wedding. That person is typically your sister, the girl you shared a room with, the girl you fought with, the girl who knew every thing about you.

Knowing that I don't have that special bond that only sisters share can be difficult at times. By the time I got married, I was so thankful to have a sister-in-law who understood what I had been through, and she was a fabulous matron of honor."

Sharing the loss of their sisters brought Meri and Ben closer together. Like any normal siblings, they still quarreled, but their losses made them realize at a young age how precious life is. Sharing the highlights of their lives became more special. "I'll never forget the huge hug he gave me after his wedding, as well as after my own wedding," Meri says. "Those are special moments that only close siblings share." She continues, "I think that when a couple loses a child at any age, the siblings tend to be forgotten. People may think the siblings are too young or do not really understand what is going on, but this is not necessarily the truth."

In addition to fathers and siblings, grandparents grieve early infant loss. They grieve particularly for their adult children's pain. "This is significant," say Henk and Margaret, who lost a grandchild. "We don't like to see our children hurt and grieving. That was and remains the deepest grief we felt. It is humbling that parents in our fallen world see their children weeping over loss of life." Henk and Margaret rejoiced to learn that their son, Stephen, and his wife, Kimberly, were expecting their second child. They immediately began including this new life in their family prayers. "We had a new member in the family," Henk says. "A soul had been created for God's honor and we were privileged to pray for him."

But at only seventeen weeks in the womb, the baby died. "Our prayers changed," Henk relates. "We pleaded for the grace of comfort and that Kimberly's life would not be threatened. We received the grace of submission, but the pain of grief was and remains a hard reality for us." On the day the baby was delivered, Henk and Margaret hurried to the hospital. They paused outside the delivery room door when they heard singing. Stephen and Kimberly sang of the Father's tender love "for all His children dear . . . Their children's children shall rejoice to see His righteousness."

"Tears filled our eyes as we heard our children's submission to the loving care of the Father," Henk and Margaret say. "God be praised for faith in Him." Henk adds, "When Malachi was brought in, we stood in awe of God's perfection of creation. "Never had we seen such a delicate, tiny human being, and he was our grandson! He was perfectly formed and beautiful to see. His tiny body fit in our hand. He weighed about five ounces and measured eight inches in length. We were amazed at the perfection of his features. The words of Psalm 139 came to mind: 'I will praise Thee for I am fearfully and wonderfully made.'"

Fathers mourn. Siblings sorrow. Grandparents grieve. Their grief may be different from that of mothers, but it can be just as painful. Acknowledge the reality of their loss. Be sensitive to a father's work behaviors or feelings. Have patience for a child's unusual questions or quirky behaviors. And express sympathy for grandparents who grieve the pain of their adult children as well as the loss of a tiny child.

Part Six: Healing Our Pain

23: Prayerful Work

Mothers and others may mourn an infant's loss. They may need to work through guilt and grief, denial and depression, anger and anxiety. It's important to remember that each individual grieves differently. Grieving parents may experience some or all of these aspects of grief with varying intensity or frequency. Some heal quickly after early infant loss; others grieve keenly for many long years.

Friends and relatives should allow mourners to grieve in their own way and time. Grieving people shouldn't try to meet the expectations of others. And they shouldn't be upset if they don't meet their own expectations. They need to allow themselves the freedom to grieve in unanticipated ways at unexpected times. They need to work through grief without forcing themselves into following a specific model. Grief isn't a straight trajectory through specific stages. Whatever its length, its intensity, or its manifestations, grief is never easy. Each individual must work through a uniquely personal set of grief issues. Grief is hard work.

The primary tool for performing this hard work is heartfelt prayer. In Psalm 50:15, God commands believers in distress to "call upon me in the day of trouble," and He promises, "I will deliver you, and you shall glorify me." God's Word may not fully penetrate the initial numbness of grief. There are times when we know God's truth in our minds, but we can't feel God's comfort in our hearts. Even forming prayers may be difficult. But God promises that His Spirit will help us in our weakness: "For we do not know what to pray for as we ought, but the Spirit himself intercedes for us with groaning too deep for words. And he who searches hearts knows what is the mind of the Spirit, because the Spirit intercedes for the saints according to the will of God" (Rom. 8:26–27). When our prayers are incoherent moans, God the Holy Spirit transforms our inarticulate groaning into prayer that accords with God's will and pleases Him. When we first begin articulating prayers, they may be limited to emotional pleas for mercy.

The Psalms are full of cries for God's grace. Psalm 102 begins with this poignant plea: "Hear my prayer, O LORD; let my cry come to you! Do not hide your face from me in the day of my distress! Incline your ear to me; answer me speedily in the day when I call! For my days pass away like smoke, and my bones burn like a furnace" (vv. 1–3). The Psalmist pleads with God for a speedy answer to his prayer. He is in such despair that he feels as if his very bones are burning away and his life is disappearing like smoke that disperses in the wind.

We know that God hears and answers the prayers of those in distress. We can pray with confidence: "For you, O LORD, are good and forgiving, abounding in steadfast love to all who call upon you. Give ear, O LORD, to my prayer; listen to my plea for grace. In the day of my trouble I call upon you, for you answer me" (Ps. 86:5–7). God not only hears and answers prayer, but He also brings healing. When Hezekiah became ill and was about to die, he prayed with bitter tears. God responded, "I have heard your prayer; I have seen your tears. Behold, I will heal you" (2 Kings 20:5).

Although God may not heal every illness, He is the source of all healing—both physical and emotional. He hears our prayers and sees our tears. He provides grace that enables us to work through the various aspects and manifestations of our grief. Prayerfully working through grief can be difficult for Christians if they have an unbalanced view of God's sovereignty that excludes His compassion. They may angrily think of Him as cold and harsh. And then they may feel guilty for being angry at God. Christian psychologist Steven Runner says, "One area that is not understood or handled well by the Christian community or the grieving Christian is the anger part of grief. Many Christians believe it's wrong to be angry, especially to be angry with God."

"Grief in response to the loss of a child will almost certainly bring out anger and doubt in relationship to God," he adds. "A lot of Christians will be in denial about this; however, when Christians repress or deny these feelings, they may still have them at their emotional core. If it's not being worked through, it can fester like a wound that's not been healed. That can lead to a longer-term bitterness or resentment toward

God. God can and does redeem grief. He can take a person from a place of anger and doubt to a place of deepened faith and trust," he emphasizes. "Avoiding that journey, however, is more likely to build up walls between the individual and God."

Dr. Runner notes that the Christian community isn't always effective in supporting those who struggle with anger toward God. "We're quick to shut that person down and defend God rather than trusting that God is big enough to handle their anger and help them heal through voicing it and processing it," he says. "Solid Christians—given the space to talk about their questions, doubts, and anger—will often, over time, come to a place where they see God's providence, accept it, and still believe that it is good." Dr. Runner believes writing letters to God or regular journaling to God can be helpful for expressing feelings, thoughts, and questions. Journaling helps grieving persons see how their grief gradually moves from the despair of anger and doubt to the hope and peace of acceptance and renewed trust.

In *A Grief Observed,* C.S. Lewis famously worked his way through intense grief following the loss of his wife. Writing as an act to create meaning, he honestly chronicled his anger at God and his doubts about God's existence and essence. When Lewis could again believe in Christ's atoning work, he began to experience relief from numbness and depression. He came to see his grief as a time of testing, but he realized that testing wasn't for God to determine the quality of Lewis's faith (God already knew that). Rather, the testing was to benefit Lewis and bring him to a fuller awareness of God. Lewis finally ordered his thinking to prioritize God first, his deceased wife next, and himself last. Only then was he able to choose an attitude of praise and thankfulness. This brief summary of *A Grief Observed* demonstrates how journaling can help a grieving person honestly work through anger and doubts. Reading *A Grief Observed* or similar accounts of grief also may help a person work through her grieving process.

Some believers may immediately find comfort and peace in God's promises. Others may struggle with pain and doubt for some time. Some may cycle back and forth between anger and acceptance. Many may need professional or pastoral counseling to help them work through their grief. All need the love and support of the Christian community and the freedom to express anger, fear, or doubt. Once the person has had sufficient opportunity to assess and voice feelings, it may be time to gently provide reminders of God's compassion. "We need to be careful not to come off too harshly or judgmentally and focus instead on understanding and empathizing," says Dr. Runner, "but we also need to remind people of the aspects of God that a person who is stuck in anger might be ignoring. It's a delicate balance."

Love is one of those important aspects. God is love (1 John 4:8, 16). He loves us and understands our grief. Jesus grieved the loss of a loved one. When facing the grave of Lazarus, "He wept" (John 11:35). As a sinless man, He grieved. Christ is divine and sits at the right hand of God, but He also remains truly human. Hebrews 4:15–16 says, "For we do not have a high priest who is unable to sympathize with our weaknesses, but one who in every respect has been tempted as we are, yet without sin. Let us then with confidence draw near to the throne of grace, that we may receive mercy and find grace to help in time of need."

24: Graceful Acceptance

As we work through hard aspects of grief, we can pray knowing that Jesus Christ understands our pain and will grant us grace. He became flesh and dwelt among us, full of grace and truth (John 1:14). From the fullness of His grace, we receive such abundant grace that John calls it "grace upon grace" (John 1:16). Paul often writes about God's grace in salvation and sanctification. Just as Paul worked hard in his ministry, we may have to work through difficult aspects of grief. But like Paul, we can say, "It was not I, but the grace of God" that was with us (1 Cor. 15:10). Paul echoes John's assessment of God's abundant grace: "And God is able to make *all* grace abound to you," so that you will have "*all* sufficiency in *all* things at *all* times" (2 Cor. 9:8–9, emphasis added).

God's grace enables believers to come to a peaceful acceptance of their loss. Many beautiful benedictions in the Bible highlight the intrinsic link between grace and peace. Galatians 1:3 is a representative example: "Grace to you and peace from God our Father and the Lord Jesus Christ." Galatians 6:18 demonstrates that this peace can be assimilated internally: "The grace of our Lord Jesus Christ be with your spirit." And Romans 16:20 links grace and peace to our victorious future: "The God of peace will soon crush Satan under your feet. The grace of our Lord Jesus Christ be with you." A peaceful God crushing Satan may seem like an oxymoron. But it comforts believers to know that God will one day grant us victory over our great enemy and all the pain he has caused in our lives. In the meantime, God equips us with His grace.

Only God's grace enables mourners to eventually arrive at the peace of acceptance. That peace is found in submission to God's will, the best example of which is Christ's prayer in the garden of Gethsemane (Matt. 26). The approaching separation from God the Father was excruciating for Christ to face. He said, "My soul is very sorrowful, even to death" (v. 38). He fell on His face and prayed, "My Father, if it be possible, let this cup pass from me; nevertheless, not as I will, but as you will" (v. 39). Christ didn't merely pray this once; He fervently prayed this heartfelt prayer three times. Then he submitted Himself to God's will. He willingly gave up his life for ours. He was forsaken by God so that we never will be.

Our submission to God's will and our acceptance of loss is attained by grace and infused with grace. But it isn't always free of pain. The old adage that time heals all wounds is true to some extent, but it might be more accurate to say that time eventually dulls the pain. Mourners shouldn't expect that their grief will grow less and less intense each day. Grieving isn't like a chart with a steadily decreasing line. It spikes up to elevated peaks and plunges down to deep valleys. Grief will become less intense over the years, but it may intensify at unexpected times. Months or years later—for no apparent reason—a person may struggle with grief that seems nearly as difficult as the initial stages. Or something may trigger a memory that stirs grief from its murky depths and makes it suddenly burst to the surface.

Patsy describes such an experience: "I was cleaning out the basement, going through some old boxes, and I actually had to close a box full of baby things from Daneil; it was too much to handle without Scott home! I set it aside to go through later, but no matter how 'better' I feel—and I really do feel content—some of the grief is there, just under the surface, coming out at odd times."

Karen says, "It is not always easy to talk about, as the memories come back to the surface if I spend too much time dwelling on the past. It goes to show that time does not heal all wounds. The pain dulls; you learn to cope and look ahead with hope, but you never forget the painful times you have had in the past."

Activity and denial may keep a person from initially experiencing the brunt of grief. Lori didn't feel the full force of her grief until Mother's Day, three months after Sarah's death. The next two months were the most difficult for her. "The whys and what-ifs were hard to get away from," she says. "I thought: Why me? Why Sarah? Why us? With all the other babies born with little or no complications or problems, why our family?"

"Time does heal," she adds, "I don't think of Sarah several times a day, but I do think of her daily. I wonder: What would she be doing now? What would she be saying? What would she look like?"

Time heals physical wounds. But many wounds retain a scar as a reminder. And some injuries cause arthritis or other pain that unexpectedly flares up for the rest of life. In a similar way, the pain of grief eventually heals. Some people recover with no visible evidence or internal pain. Others recall the pain as often as they would see a scar on their hand. And like the gnawing pain of arthritis that intensifies with certain weather conditions, some experience deeply rooted and recurring pain for the rest of their lives.

The wound of grief could be considered healed when one comes to acceptance. That acceptance is *grace-full* because it's possible only by God's grace and because it is full of God's grace. But it is also *graceful* because it is a response of submission to God's will characterized by grace, evidenced in a beautiful attitude of trust.

By God's grace, Amanda came to a graceful acceptance of her childless state. In seeing this acceptance grow in her life, she witnessed God's transforming power. She says, "What a blessing it is to be able to say that God transformed the pain in my life into something beautiful for His glory and honor!"

Also by God's grace, Bonnie has learned to live with the loss of childlessness and even has found her faith strengthened. "The way Christ has given me His grace over the years has been through His chosen means: the Word, the sacraments, and prayer," she says. "God sees my need, He knows my frame, He provides for everything I could ever want or ask for, through these means. He builds my faith, He sustains my life, and He is my precious Savior. He does not give me anything I cannot bear. Sometimes He takes me to the limit, but He never goes beyond. My life is His, His is mine. His glory is much more important than any short-term worldly hope I may have here on earth. This life is temporary; God's glory is eternal! To God be the glory forever and ever. Amen."

Bonnie's testimony reflects the words of 1 Peter 5:9–11, a marvelous passage packed with comfort and hope. It urges believers to stand firm in their faith, knowing that others throughout the world suffer similar struggles. Reminding us of the temporary nature of suffering and the eternal nature of our future glory, it urges us to resist the devil and stand strong in the faith: "Resist him, firm in your faith, knowing that the same kinds of suffering are being experienced by your brotherhood throughout the world. And after you have suffered a little while, the God of all grace, who has called you to his eternal glory in Christ, will himself restore, confirm, strengthen, and establish you. To him be the dominion forever and ever. Amen."

25: Remembering Life

There are many ways that parents and other relatives can remember the lives of the little ones they've lost. But they may initially feel confused about how to remember their little child. They may be alone at home. They may be in the sterile surroundings of a hospital. Or they may suddenly confront loss in a totally alien environment.

Tim and Francine tragically and traumatically lost an infant during the eleventh week of pregnancy in a gas station restroom. In spite of their confusion and shock, they were able to save the baby's remains. They named the child Noah, since that name can be used for either a boy or girl (see Gen. 5:28 and Num. 27:1). "We love the meaning: 'rest,'" they say. "Psalm 62 really resonated with us as a result: 'My soul finds rest in God alone; my salvation comes from him'" (v. 1, NIV84). Psalm 62 was one of the Scripture passages family members read at a memorial service for Noah in the garden of Tim's parents. Francine had sewn a tiny blanket and embroidered *NOAH* on it, which was used to wrap the baby's body and gestational sack. Before the service, Francine took pictures of the blanket with a model of an infant in the womb at eleven weeks beside her open Bible.

Following the winter funeral, the family marked Noah's grave with flagstone, intending to plant flowers there in the spring. Francine carried the infant model in her pocket for some time, often pulling it out to help people visualize Noah. She also wrote a poem chronicling her journey from the joy of anticipating life through the trauma and pain of loss to the tearful coexistence of grief and Christian hope.

Some parents may be floundering in their first experience of loss and may have no idea what to do about funeral planning. "The feeling of 'loss' was foreign to me," Bonnie says. "I didn't really know what to do with it. It was unknown territory. Even though we didn't have a funeral, it felt as if it would have been appropriate if we had."

Those facing sudden infant loss may seek immediate guidance. Pastors and other counselors should familiarize themselves with local ordinances regarding burials and become acquainted with area funeral homes and their procedures. They then can provide better counsel to parents regarding specific options. Most obstetric departments have experience with such losses and demonstrate sensitivity toward grieving parents. Some hospitals provide counseling and care for grieving families. The family may receive a keepsake box containing information on grieving or a meaningful poem, and mementos such as a small blanket, cap, or booties. These things help parents focus on life—however brief—instead of death.

Patsy and Scott credit "compassionate hospital staff" with helping them acknowledge and cope with their losses. They were encouraged to name their babies, wrap them in blankets, hold them, and take pictures. "These things were difficult," Scott admits, "but they made the loss 'valid' and real. They were tremendously helpful."

It can be difficult for a mother to stay in an obstetrics department after the loss of a child. Karen relates that she was "haunted" by the cries of newborn babies, the laughter of grandparents, and other celebrations of life. She winced every time the hospital played a song over the intercom indicating that a new baby had been born. But the hospital was helpful in other ways. Instead of providing a death certificate, the hospital presented Karen and Jeff with a "Certificate of Life."

Before Stephanie's induction began, the hospital provided a counselor to speak to her and Brad about planning a funeral. This was difficult for them because they still couldn't accept the fact that Caleb had died. The following day, however, they found themselves miraculously sustained when they went to the funeral home to finalize arrangements. They wanted the service to focus on the first question and answer of the Heidelberg Catechism[1] as a witness to the hope of the gospel. "We looked at this as an opportunity for friends and loved ones to hear the good news of Christ's saving work," says Brad. "We wished to challenge those we love whether Christ was indeed their only hope in life and death."

---

1. See first paragraph of chapter 17.

The time immediately following a loss or funeral quickly passes, and parents soon find themselves alone, trying to make their way through the grieving process. "The next days, and two months really, passed in a blur," Lori says. "I spent a lot of time looking through pictures, comparing Sarah with Matthew. I looked through all of Matthew's stages in scrapbooks. I did Sarah's baby book and some scrapbook pages for her. I also displayed all of the gifts we received for her."

Many parents make scrapbooks or memory boxes. Some parents plant flowering shrubs or trees in memory of the child they lost. Some wear "precious feet" lapel pins. But years later, questions may remain and physical reminders may be painful. "I have a large plastic sweater box under my bed full of Caleb's memories," Stephanie says. "I rarely look through it because it is still just so painful. We even have a tape of the funeral that we have never listened to or viewed. We seldom visit the gravesite in a children's section of the cemetery. It is so difficult to go there and see the toy cars, baby dolls, and stuffed animals that others have left. We do talk about Caleb with our children, and I have a picture of him by my bedside."

"As Joshua (15 months older than Caleb would have been) continues to grow, I long to see the boys together! They would be on the same baseball team, soccer team, and in Boy Scouts together. Caleb's absence is so profound in my life. Since we never had another son, Joshua will never have a living brother. As his three sisters play together, he is often left out (not too interested in tea parties and baby dolls!). I sometimes wonder: Would a brother straighten out a few behavioral issues he has? If I did not trust in God's sovereignty and his graciousness in Christ, I would have no comfort or hope."

Some parents find themselves preoccupied with thoughts of heaven. "I thought a lot about dying and heaven," Lori says. "I had never thought much about this subject, but I now found it intriguing. The most comforting thing to me is that God is always with me, and Sarah is being cared for by One greater than I. She will never know the pains of this world. She will never have an earache or a broken heart." God was doubly gracious to Randy and Lori by blessing them later with the birth of twins: a boy and a girl. But the couple still remembers Sarah and how God used her. "Sarah's picture hangs with those of her brothers and sister," Lori says. "Sarah taught me to trust in God. She taught me that I am stronger, only with God's help, than I ever thought possible."

Couples blessed with subsequent children find them a precious joy in themselves, but also a bittersweet reminder of the life lost. "I still have moments when I stand back and watch our son Josiah as he plays," Karen says. "It is hard to believe that he is the same little boy we fought so hard to save. It can also be bittersweet; this little child has a twin that we never met. Every time Josiah reaches a milestone, we remember our other child, and we wonder what he or she would have been like at this same age. Josiah is a constant reminder of God's grace in giving him to us, but also of the loss we endured." In whatever ways parents remember the children they've lost, they can know that God keeps their memory constantly before Him since their names are engraved on the palms of His hands (Isa. 49:16).

26: Compassionate Care

How can you help those grieving the loss of an infant? Job's comforters started well. They wept, tore their robes, sprinkled dust on their heads, and—because they saw his suffering was so intense—they sat with him on the ground for seven days and seven nights without saying a word (Job 2:11–13). These specific actions demonstrated their compassion and their solidarity with Job's suffering. It can be difficult to know what to say to a grieving person, but it may not always be necessary to say something. Hugs and tears convey more than words. Sympathetic listening may mean more than eloquent speaking.

During her initial grief, Karen particularly appreciated visits. The visit itself mattered more to her than what people said. "One that particularly stands out in my mind was from a man who didn't say much," she says, "but simply sat with me and cried."

Greg and Bonnie received great comfort when an elder visited them. "One of our elders from church came and prayed with us," Bonnie says. "This was very important and comforting to us. We were brought to the throne room of grace at a time when we felt like it was a very difficult thing for us to do on our own." The best comforters may be those who simply show up, sit with the mourners, cry with them, and pray with them. They are present when they are needed and show that they are hurting with the grieving parents.

Job's friends failed as comforters when they began blaming his misfortunes on his own sin. Like those accusatory comforters, modern comforters sometimes say the wrong things. There are several things that are not helpful to say to grieving parents:

"You can always have another child." (Even if that may be possible, they are grieving an irreplaceable child.)

"At least you have other children." (Being grateful for existing children doesn't diminish the pain of this loss.)

"There probably was something wrong, and this was for the best." (You don't know this, and their current pain doesn't feel like "the best" for them.)

"What caused it?" (They likely don't have an answer, and this may generate guilt or create further questions in their minds.)

"How far along were you?" (This question may imply that an early loss is less significant than a later loss.)

"I know just how you feel." (Even if you've had a miscarriage, you do not know exactly how this person feels. Every grief experience is unique.)

It's more helpful to convey genuine sympathy and offer specific assistance:

"I'm so sorry for the loss of your child." (Acknowledge the baby's personhood.)

"I'm sure this is very difficult for you." (Acknowledge the sufferer's pain.)

"I'm here if you need to talk to someone." (Be a compassionate listener.)

"I'll call you next Tuesday to see how you're doing." (Being specific and following through is more effective than simply saying, "Call me if you need me.")

"Would you like me to bring a meal on Monday, come over on Saturday to help clean the house, take you out to lunch on Wednesday?" (Specific offers are better than the vague, "Let me know what I can do to help.")

If parents are struggling with difficult medical conditions, avoid asking for details. They may not want to describe procedures or talk about decisions. Rather than asking personal questions, allow them to share the amount of information they want to reveal. Although God may well use this experience to help grieving parents minister to others suffering similar losses in the future, it isn't helpful to tell them that is the reason they suffer now. And although we know the Lord "disciplines those he loves" (Prov. 3:12, NIV84), telling this to someone who grieves can heap pain and guilt on their grief, making them wonder what they have done that requires God's discipline.

Sometimes people avoid talking about a loss because they don't know what to say or don't want to remind sufferers of their grief and make them break into tears. But grieving persons always think about their loss. Your failure to mention it may seem like ignoring the loss and may hurt worse than saying something. Simply asking, "How are you doing?" conveys concern and gives the grieving person freedom to express feelings. "The best advice I could give would be to acknowledge the death of the baby, to mention the baby's name if possible," says Patsy. "Although it was not the only thing that we could or wanted to talk about—it was terribly painful when people ignored our loss."

"I really cannot stress enough that it is important to acknowledge the loss," she adds. "Ignoring the loss is devastating to the one whose life has completely changed. Saying, 'I like that name you chose for your baby,' goes beyond a simple condolence and opens the door for the grieving parent to talk about it, if they choose."

One friend shared with Stephanie that her son Caleb had perfectly fulfilled God's entire plan for him. That comforted her, since she was focusing on all Caleb had missed. "That gave me a more biblical perspective on God's sovereignty and His plan," says Stephanie. "Another woman commented on our sons' names: 'Oh, Caleb has just entered the Promised Land a bit before Joshua!' That one still brings a smile to my face."

Lori says, "The best advice I can think of is, let the person know you care and you will be available when they are ready to talk—if ever. Finding someone with a similar experience is very helpful to compare stories and share feelings."

This discussion of sensitive speech needs to include consideration for those who do not have children. A childless couple may be trying hard to have children. Questions like, "When are you going to start a family?" can be extremely painful. Amanda, who suffered much from such callousness, notes that the experience has made her a more compassionate person: "I am far less judgmental, and I choose my words more carefully, because I know how much an innocent question can hurt."

Think about things you can do to express your sympathy. A bouquet of flowers can show that you are thinking about and praying for the grieving parents. Grieving parents appreciate cards conveying sympathy, especially if they include personal notes mentioning the baby, by name if possible. Personal letters may be even more meaningful than purchased cards. "Within days of the miscarriage," Bonnie says, "a couple sent us beautiful, heartfelt, and tenderly written letters. They had gone through similar experiences with infertility and truly empathized with us. They gave our emotional 'heartbreak' legitimacy."

Bonnie relates that such expressions of sympathy helped the couple feel as if their grief was "real" and that they weren't "just weak people." She says, "We had truly experienced something catastrophic, and we needed extra grace, comfort, and understanding from those around us. These dear ones were given to us by God to bring a cup of cool water for our needy souls."

Perhaps you are able to make a gift for the grieving parents. One of Patsy's sisters gave her a poem with Daneil's name in calligraphy, which conveyed a Christian message. Another sister cross-stitched each baby's name, birth date, and a portion of the funeral text. Those pieces still hang prominently in Scott and Patsy's living room.

Try to avoid setting expectations for when grieving parents ought to be past grief. Don't expect them and don't tell them to "just get over it." Karen recommends reading a book about infant loss to help you minister to others, then keeping extra copies on hand so that you have one to give to parents who lose a child. She suggests that it not be too harsh, stressing God's discipline and the need to "toughen up," but rather emphasizing the desperately needed comfort of God. She says, "I found that being able to read a book during the quiet times when I was alone with my Savior was very helpful."

Stephanie reminds grieving parents of God's sovereignty: "God is in control of every minute detail of your life. Your baby did not die accidentally; there was nothing you could have done to save your baby. God is with you in this tremendous pain; you are not alone. Rest in the sovereignty of God and His love and care for His own. He will restore your soul and fill the void in your life with Himself."

27: The Hope in My Heart

The seventy-year-old woman who knits baby blankets works through her grief over the child she couldn't hold because it was whisked away and her miscarriage was not discussed. The mom who crafts a scrapbook finds solace in creating something concrete for the daughter whose hair she never brushed and tied with ribbons. The mother who plants the tree sees it grow and remembers the life she never saw blossom. This discussion of infant loss began with my own story of loss. It continued by describing society's split personality regarding infant loss and showing from Scripture the significance of such losses. An overview of losses throughout history brought the discussion to modern times and the common occurrence of loss. Several families shared their personal stories, including stories of infertility and adoption. The focus then turned to the comfort possible for grieving Christians (including mothers, fathers, siblings, and grandparents). Christ's comfort is possible even for those whose grief is complicated by guilt or the need for forgiveness. Discussions on working through grief, finding peace in acceptance, remembering life, and helping the grieving brought us to this point.

This discussion of infant loss concludes with my own affirmation of hope. The littlest lambs are not lost. The Good Shepherd gathers them in His arms and gently leads their parents beside peaceful still waters into hopeful green pastures. Christians should not be afraid to call a baby a baby. Let's recognize that a child at any point in the pregnancy is a creation of God. Let's not fall prey to a pro-abortion mindset that minimizes pre-term loss. Let's reach out to dads, siblings, and grandparents as well as moms in acknowledging their losses. Let's continue ministering to our hurting sisters and brothers long after the initial pain. And let's humbly realize that the reason why God, in His infinite wisdom, chooses to end a life before it really begins is beyond our finite understanding.

In the first chapter of this book, I described my joy in the birth of a precious and healthy daughter after experiencing difficulties during that pregnancy. As I write this final chapter, that daughter is a happily married young woman who recently gave birth to her first child: a healthy baby boy. The years between those two pregnancies have gone so fast that they give a glimpse of God's perspective of time. To Him a thousand years are like a three-hour watch in the night. If you're the sleepy watchman, who'd rather be wrapped in a cozy blanket, three hours seem long. If you're in painful labor, three hours seem very long. But even for the sleepy watchman or the eager mother, three hours soon pass.

Writing this book has been a long and difficult process. It was difficult to find adequate time, viable organization, and appropriate words. In addition to these practical problems, there were huge emotional hurdles. Writing this manuscript forced me to face my own fears and failings, and brought me to previously unknown levels of dependence, humility, and trust.

But more important, it has taken me alongside many brave couples who courageously shared their very private and poignant stories. Infant loss is an emotional subject; it has been heartrending to visit and revisit these personal stories of loss. These parents have taken time to share their stories, opening their hearts and reopening their partially healed wounds. They didn't want to increase their pain, but they did want to somehow help others who have lost little ones. It is my prayer that their efforts will be worth the emotional pain, that some grieving parents will benefit from this work, that someone will better understand infant loss, or that someone will be better equipped to minister to grieving families. Above all, it is my prayer that through this work, as in all I do, God is glorified.

Throughout this difficult process, it has been good to be reminded of the Christian's comfort in Christ and hope for the future. No matter how traumatic the loss, no matter how much or how little it is grieved, believers have hope of a glorious future. We look to that future with hope that is firmly based on God's sure promises for a future free from pain and sorrow. Our future existence will not be as vague spirits floating in the clouds. When Christ returns, we—and our covenant children—will be reunited with our original bodies, glorified in a way far beyond our imaginings. God the Father sent His Son to atone for all our sins. He sends His Spirit to comfort us in our sorrows. He sustains us during all our trials. He equips us to every task He places before us. He will fill our hearts with peace, even in times of deepest despair. He holds before us the hope of an existence free from grief and full of joy.

Women who grieve the loss of a child they never conceived, fathers who grieve the loss of a son they never held, grandparents who grieve for their adult children's pain, and mothers who grieve a child while still suffering the sad effects of abuse may never find complete and comprehensive healing on earth. They can know, however, that there is no grief in glory. "For I consider that the sufferings of this present time are not worth comparing with the glory that is to be revealed to us" (Rom. 8:18). "But, as it is written, 'What no eye has seen, nor ear heard, nor the heart of man imagined, what God has prepared for those who love him" (1 Cor. 2:9). No matter how heavy and long our losses seem in this earthly realm, they are light and momentary in eternal reality (2 Cor. 4:17). We live now by faith, not by sight (2 Cor. 5:7). But one day soon, at our Lord's glorious appearing, the curtain of our burden will lift and our faith will at last become sight.

Appendix: Medical Terms

Parents may hear various medical terms used to describe their loss. *Antenatal* or *antepartum death* occurs before labor. *Intranatal* or *intrapartum death* occurs during labor. *Perinatal mortality* includes deaths from the age of viability through seven days after delivery. *Neonatal mortality* includes deaths in the first twenty-eight days after delivery, and may be further divided into *early neonatal mortality* (the first seven days) and *late neonatal mortality* (before twenty-nine days). *Post-neonatal mortality* is defined as deaths after twenty-eight days but before one year.

I use the term *pregnancy* in this book to mean the time—from the moment of conception—that a baby is within its mother's womb. Although this use may seem vague, since the moment of conception is impossible to pinpoint, I use *pregnancy* rather than *gestation*, which seems insensitive. The National Vital Statistics System (NVSS) defines *gestation* as "beginning with the first day of the last normal menstrual period and ending with the day of birth or day of termination of pregnancy."

Infrequently, I use the term *embryo* in this book to refer to a tiny baby in the earliest stages of pregnancy. It is defined as from conception to about the eighth week.

The term *fetus* is defined as from about the eighth week after conception until birth. Although it is a legitimate and accurate term to use, I avoid it in this book because it is frequently used in pro-abortion rhetoric to deny personhood of the unborn.

An *ectopic pregnancy* is a pregnancy in which the fertilized egg implants anywhere other than the uterus, most frequently in a fallopian tube.

I prefer the term *miscarriage* to the term *spontaneous abortion;* it indicates a loss during pregnancy before the possibility of survival (also known as *viability*). Miscarriage is usually defined as up to about the twentieth week (which is half way through a normal pregnancy), although the distinction is sometimes considered as being between twenty and twenty-four weeks. Medical terms used for very early miscarriages, occurring before the sixth week after the last menstrual period, are *early pregnancy loss* or *chemical pregnancy* or *preclinical pregnancy.* Bleeding during pregnancy may indicate a possible miscarriage and is medically known as a *threatened abortion.* The extremely insensitive term *habitual aborter* may be used to refer to a woman who has experienced multiple miscarriages.

Other related terms parents may encounter are *incomplete abortion* or *missed abortion,* referring to a miscarriage in which the baby, placenta, or other elements are not naturally expelled. This generally requires either a D&C (Dilation and Curettage) or D&E (Dilation and Evacuation—sometimes called Dilation and Extraction) medical procedure. A D&C is usually performed before the twelfth week of pregnancy and involves dilation of the cervix and either scraping or suctioning remaining tissue from the wall of the uterus. A D&E is generally performed between the fourteenth and twentieth week of pregnancy; it involves dilation of the cervix and removal of the baby and placenta. An alternative to this procedure might be induced labor, which would allow the parents to view and hold the baby.

Although *abortion* technically means any termination of pregnancy, the term has become conditioned by culture to mean an intentional termination. In this book, it indicates an intentional action at any time during pregnancy, before or after viability.

The term *viability* indicates the stage of development at which a child may be able to live and grow outside the womb. Increasing research is being done regarding the viability of extremely premature infants born between twenty-two and twenty-five weeks (known as "the threshold of viability"); however, the generally accepted view remains that viability begins around twenty-four weeks.

Stillbirth indicates the delivery of a child, after the age of viability, who has died from natural causes while in the womb. Various sources restrict the meaning of the term only to vaginal deliveries (as opposed to surgical) or only to losses after twenty weeks. The United Kingdom legally defines *stillbirth* as loss after twenty-four weeks. Canada and the United States are abandoning the term *stillbirth* for the term *fetal death*, which the World Health Organization (WHO) defined in 1950 as "death prior to the complete expulsion or extraction from its mother of a product of human conception, irrespective of the duration of pregnancy and which is not an induced termination of pregnancy." The term *fetal death* seems less specific and less sensitive than referring to early loss as *miscarriage* and later loss as *stillbirth*, especially considering the abortion industry language of the WHO definition ("product of conception" and "induced termination"). Occasionally stillbirth may be referred to as "Sudden Antenatal Death Syndrome" or SADS (*antenatal* is Latin for "before birth"). Used similarly to Sudden Infant Death Syndrome or SIDS (which is the sudden loss of an infant with no apparent cause), SADS is defined as the sudden death of a "fetus" with no apparent cause.

The term *premature* refers to a baby born a few weeks before its due date. It is generally defined as being before the thirty-seventh week. The term *newborn* means a recently-born infant. The medical term for an infant during the first month of life is *neonate*. Newborns include those born prematurely, those born full term, or those born after their due date. The term *infant* usually indicates a child during the first year outside the womb.

Special thanks to Dr. David A. Kreuze of West Michigan Obstetricians and Gynecologists, who specializes in high risk pregnancy and infertility, for helpfully reviewing the above medical terminology.

Note to the Reader

The publisher invites you to respond to us about this book by writing Reformed Fellowship, Inc., 3500 Danube Dr. SW, Grandville, MI 49418-8387 USA. You may also email us at *president@reformedfellowship.net*

Founded in 1951, Reformed Fellowship is a religious and strictly nonprofit organization composed of a group of Christian believers who hold to the biblical Reformed faith. Our purpose is to advocate and propagate this faith, to nurture those who seek to live in obedience to it, to give sharpened expression to it, to stimulate the doctrinal sensitivities of those who profess it, to promote the spiritual welfare and purity of the Reformed churches, and to encourage Christian action.

Members of Reformed Fellowship express their adherence to the Calvinistic creeds as formulated in the Belgic Confession, the Heidelberg Catechism, the Canons of Dort, and the Westminster Confession and Catechisms.

To fulfill our mission, we publish a bi-monthly journal, *The Outlook*, and we publish books and Bible study guides. Our website is *www.reformedfellowship.net*